The Entire Earth and Sky

LESLIE CAROL ROBERTS

UNIVERSITY OF NEBRASKA PRESS | LINCOLN & LONDON

The Entire Earth and Sky
Views on Antarctica

The essay "Entire Earth and Sky" was originally published in *On Nature: Great Writers on the Great Outdoors*, Lee Gutkind, ed. (New York: Jeremy P. Tarcher/Putnam, a member of the Putnam Penguin Group, 2002). © 2002.

Library of Congress Cataloging-in-Publication Data
Roberts, Leslie Carol. The entire earth and sky : views on Antarctica / Leslie Carol Roberts.
p.   cm.   Includes bibliographical references.
ISBN 978-0-8032-1617-4 (cloth : alk. paper)
1. Antarctica—History. 2. Antarctica—Discovery and exploration. 3. Roberts, Leslie Carol—Travel —Antarctica. I. Title.
G870.R59 2008   919.8'9—dc22   2008011315

Set in Quadraat by Bob Reitz. Designed by R. W. Boeche.

May 2009

For my beloved children, Will and Helena

I think I could stop here myself and do miracles.
—Walt Whitman

It is a commonplace of all religious thought, even the most primitive, that the man seeking visions and insight must go apart from his fellows and live for a time in the wilderness. If he is of the proper sort, he will return with a message. It may not be a message from the god he set out to seek, but even if he has failed in that particular, he will have had a vision or seen a marvel, and these are always worth listening to and thinking about.

— Loren Eiseley, The Judgment of Birds

Ice.

Ice is.

Ice is nice.

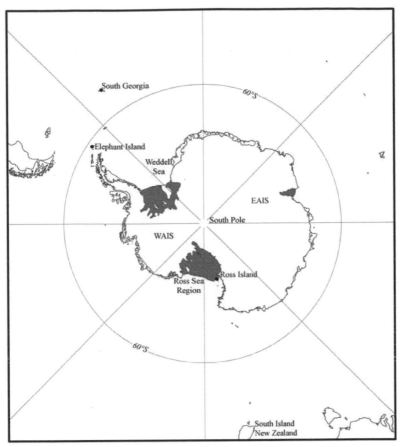

Map of Antarctica, depicting the Ross Sea Region (note its close proximity to New Zealand's South Island), the West Antarctic Ice Sheet, and the East Antarctic Ice Sheet. Elephant Island and South Georgia are included to illustrate the start and stop points for Frank Arthur Worsley's 800-mile small boat journey. Courtesy of Irfon Jones, Gateway Antarctica.

An Antarctican Gazetteer

Please note: The details and facts, circumstances and encoun-
ters included in this list came together over time with the
help, swiftness, and assurance of my children, Will and Helena, provisional Antarctic experts in their own right, and in
it we sought to establish the minutiae and vastness of the
Antarctic continent and what it means to us. We selected
these facts from among tens of millions at our disposal.
We recorded many of these facts during scientific lectures
or when watching films about Antarctica or when reading
aloud from our mountainous Antarctic library. A key dis-
claimer must be inserted at this point: While our process
could be described as random, it could also be considered
deliberate, given that we see history and the earth sciences
as foundational collages. The privileging of some facts over
others, and the reasons behind these hierarchies, is never
far from our minds. Specifically, we rarely separate ideas
about "people" from "landscape." We also see all ideas on
"ice" as different categorically from "habitation habits." If you

prefer more familiar information baskets, this may not be the section for you, and in which case we advise you to skip these pages entirely. The fact is many readers have made it quite happily to this point knowing very little about Antarctica. You could also fill in by visiting the Central Intelligence Agency's Web site, where you will find a method of recording place that some will find thorough and informative but that others may judge synthetic and pure fiction. Like all data collection, the CIA's method does introduce misunderstanding, and while we do not want to cast any shadow on our colleagues in research and facts in the U.S. government, we would be doing no one a favor to remain silent. Antarctica, for instance, is reported as having no arable land. We believe this is inaccurate and plan to file a complaint when we return from our current explorations.

There are no indigenous Antarcticans

The CIA World Factbook offers this rank-order list:
World 510,072,000 square kilometers
Pacific Ocean 155,557,000
Atlantic Ocean 76,762,000
Indian Ocean 68,556,000
Southern Ocean 20,327,000
Russia 17,075,200
Arctic Ocean 14,056,000
Antarctica 14,000,000
Canada 9,984,670
United States 9,631,418

It is the only continent where all people compete on an annual basis for the chance to reside and work there and where you need no official documentation to "prove" who you are. When you arrive, they have been expecting you.

Twenty-six nations have stations and people on the ice, including Great Britain, the United States, Russia, France, Australia, Argentina, New Zealand, and China. Thirteen Belgians, eighty Brazilians, and sixteen Bulgarians also make residence on the ice.

When winter's twenty-four-hour darkness descends, the community shrinks from four thousand to one thousand. (The continental population in summer is equal to that of Sioux County, North Dakota.)

Antarctica was once the center of the Gondwana supercontinent, which included Africa, India, South America, and Australia. As the continents drifted apart, ocean water surrounded Antarctica. The Earth's rotation caused the West Wind Drift with its clockwise movement, thus isolating the continent from warmer northerly weather and water. Because of this, ice crept across Antarctica about 40 million years ago and has remained largely intact since then.

Ninety-eight percent of the continent is covered by ice, with a volume of 30 million cubic kilometers. At the South Pole the ice is 2.8 kilometers thick. The ice's weight has depressed continental bedrock by 600 meters.

Although Antarctica contains 70 percent of the Earth's fresh water in the form of ice, the continental interior averages less than five centimeters of rain a year, making Antarctica as dry as the Sahara desert.

On November 29, 1929, Rear Admiral Richard E. Byrd of the U.S. Navy became the first to fly over the South Pole for the first time.

In 1956 the American doctor Paul Siple and seventeen

colleagues wintered at the South Pole while conducting experiments for the International Geophysical Year. The South Pole has had residents every year since then.

A group of five Norwegian men were the first to stand at the South Pole. They arrived on December 14, 1911, and have been lauded for doing so by traveling light and moving fast. Led by the formidable Roald Amundsen, they covered 1,860 miles in ninety-nine days.

Sir James Ross penetrated the pack ice in 1841 and discovered the ice shelf that now carries his name. This ice shelf is the size of France or Texas.

Satellite images of Antarctica's seasonally changing ice shelves are collages, mosaics, made from images shot throughout the year.

Ice tongues are projections from shelves or glaciers formed by wind and ocean currents. They can project several kilometers into the sea.

Under ice shelves, a thick carpet of phytoplankton find a desirably isolated haven. Nearby, where the ice peels back from the shoreline, sea anemones, sea cucumbers, starfish, soft corals, and sea urchins find the cold to their liking as well. A limpet, a type of snail, scoots along, providing kelp gulls with their daily supply of calcium and protein.

Antarctica's minerals continue to capture miners' imaginations. Lead, gold, copper, and silver reside in the Antarctic Peninsula. The Pensacola Mountains are thought to hold chromium and platinum. Low-grade coal has been found in the Transantarctics. Deposits of oil and natural gas are believed to exist in sedimentary basins far below the Ross and Weddell Seas.

Wind velocities at Commonwealth Bay have been recorded at 180 miles per hour.

> There are four South Poles. The geographic is at the southern end of the Earth's rotational axis, where lines of longitude converge. This is where they plant the flags. The magnetic is where lines of the Earth's magnetic field converge. The geomagnetic is a theoretical point marking the southern end of the Earth's geomagnetic field. The Pole of Relative Inaccessibility is the place farthest, in all directions, from both coastlines.

The magnetic South Pole shifts and floats a few kilometers a year as the Earth's magnetic field changes.

> The Antarctic Convergence is where Antarctic surface water—cold and relatively low in salinity—meets the relatively warmer sub-Antarctic surface water. The colder water sinks as it flows northward and plays a major role in governing Earth's climate.

The Southern Ocean is the body of water lying south of the Antarctic Convergence and covers about 13,500 square miles or 10 percent of the world's oceans. It is the coldest, densest ocean on the planet and has the highest biological productivity of all the oceans.

> The Antarctic Circle is located at 66 degrees 33 seconds and marks the northern limit of the region—in this place, the sun does not set at the southern hemisphere's summer solstice, on or about December 22, nor rise at the winter solstice, on or about June 21. The precise location of the Antarctic Circle shifts year to year because the Earth shimmies on its axis ever so slightly.

Some three hundred species of algae live along Antarctic coasts. Lichens and mosses have been found inland—at last count, two hundred types of lichens, eighty-five mosses, and two types of flowering plants reside on the Antarctic continent.

> The Leopard seal is an aggressive predator who eats penguins, fish, krill, and is not adverse to hunting people. In recent years, a Leopard seal attacked and drowned a British scientist. Their only predator is the killer whale, or orca.

Southern right whales are fifty-eight feet long and weigh one hundred tons. They got their name because they were the "right" ones to kill. Oil laden and floatable when killed, by the end of the nineteenth century the right whale was nearly extinct.

> Minke whales, at twenty-six to thirty feet long and weighing ten tons, are the blue whale's tiniest cousins. About two hundred thousand live in the Antarctic, nearly half the world's population. The Japanese hunt minke whales and then sell their meat to delighted consumers at home.

Orcas, called killer whales, are the largest members of the dolphin family. They hunt cooperatively across the world's oceans. Orcas put on a show when pack hunting, and have been documented riding waves onto Antarctic beaches in order to snatch unsuspecting seals from their slumber.

> Krill are found in abundance around Antarctica and form the foundation of the food chain. They directly or indirectly feed seals, fish, squid, penguins, and other sea birds. Japanese and Russian trawlers harvest hundreds of thousands of tons of krill a year.

Chinstrap penguins get their name from a thin black

line running under their chins. They stand about twenty-seven inches tall and weigh in at nine pounds.

The earliest reference to penguins was logged in 1499 by Vasco de Gama's expedition to India. In 1519 Magellan recorded South American penguins.

Penguins don't live in the Northern Hemisphere because they cannot tolerate warm ocean temperatures. They have never lived in the Arctic, and all drawings depicting polar bears and penguins on the same ice floe are hideously inaccurate. Polar bears would make a tasty repast of penguins.

Adélie penguins are thirty inches tall and weigh eleven pounds. They are my family's favorite penguin, offering a crisply delineated black back and white belly. Along with the emperor penguins, they are the only "true" Antarctic penguin, defined by the fact that they actually breed in Antarctica. They are the most abundant of all the penguins even though they have a breeding season that lasts but a few short weeks.

More than nine thousand meteorite fragments have been found in the Antarctic ice sheet.

Antarctica is the fifth-largest continent and the only one covered by ice. Of its 14 million total square kilometers, only an estimated 280,000 are ice-free.

New subglacial lakes are being inventoried. Each lake may offer its own unique microcosmic stew; estimates of how many lakes exist under the ice top four hundred.

The ice itself may have its own metabolism. Scientists looking at this have said this means the entire ice sheet may be alive.

There are more engineering projects currently underway than at any other time in Antarctic history—including a new, U.S.-built, $135-million South Pole station.

> There is no standard time in Antarctica. Most countries use their home time. You can imagine the confusion this causes at places like tiny King George Island where the Chinese are near the Chileans and their "home" time zones differ by eleven hours. Why is it set up this way? During four months of summer, the sun never sets; during the same period in winter, it never rises. A clock with its twelve-hour cycles simply doesn't apply. Standardized time is designed to get everyone to the train station on time. But when there is no train . . . ?

The Earth's lowest known land that is not under the sea is in Antarctica's Bentley Subglacial Trench. No one knows what lives down there.

> Antarctic weather is a story of wind. Antarctica is the windiest of all the continents. Katabatic, or gravity-driven, wind, screams out to the coast from the center. Cyclones that form over the coast then march in a clockwise parade around the continent. Dr. Luke Copland, polar glaciologist and Antarctican, described the experience: "Imagine sitting in a car for three days with the radio stuck between stations, volume turned all the way up."

In February 2005 I traveled to Antarctica as a voyageur, aboard the *Professor Molchanov*, a fine ship once in the employ of the Russian science agency. At dinner with my mainly European cohorts, the talk spanned where everyone traveled when not in Antarctica. I have been around the world three times but could hardly keep up with this group. The most popular destination appeared to be Bhutan. All ten people at our dinner table, save me, had been to Bhutan in the previous year.

In November 2007 the first large-scale tourist disaster: the M/V Explorer hits ice and sinks in twenty hours off the coast of the Antarctic Peninsula. No one in the Antarctic travel business—explorers, scientists, operators, for instance—found this surprising in the least. All have been waiting, in fact, for this to happen. Why? Very tricky place to run a ship, according to ice pilots and seasoned Antarctic sailors. The photo of her red hull listing into ice-choked waters captured the news for a few days. All 150 passengers and crew were picked up by ships responding to their SOS. Later, we learned what was described as a "small piece" of ice had pierced the Explorer's hull.

The largest number of travelers to Antarctica at present is voyageurs: tourists who take research or cruise ships down south to look around; the number is rising more than 10 percent each year. In 2006–2007, hailed as a "record-breaking year" by Antarctic tour operators, 37,552 voyageurs traveled to the Antarctic. Of these, approximately 29,576 hit the shore, another 7,000 traveled there on boats but did not go ashore, and 1,050 paid for land-based excursions, that is, climbing ice peaks, snowboarding, and camping. In addition, 1,600 overflew the continent on large planes (737s and 747s) at approximately two thousand feet.

Puns: Antarctic ice became "breaking news." The Guardian (UK) flashes out reports on the world's largest floating object, an iceberg called B-15A, which parked off Ross Island beginning in 2000. The head of Antarctica New Zealand, an affable man named Lou Sanson, was quoted, "We know very little about what makes this thing tick." B-15A was once 1,200 square miles in size and contained enough water to supply the Nile River for eighty years.

The Ross Dependency is managed by workers at a New Zealand government subsidiary called Antarctica New Zealand. They also manage an Antarctic science museum at the Christchurch airport, where they have both a "cold room" filled with artificial snow and a "wind experience" room. A museum guide told us, "Neither replicates Antarctica's most famed, extreme conditions as this would be hazardous to museum visitors, many of whom are schoolchildren."

The number 1 selling item at gift shops in the Ross Dependency are women's string-bikini underpants.

In 2002 the Larsen B Ice Shelf collapsed and dispersed in a matter of days. The Larsen B was the size of Rhode Island. Scientists have confirmed that rising global temperatures contribute to the break up of ice shelves around the Antarctic Peninsula. This has been compared to breaking a crust off a pie—then watching the insides run out of the pan. Ice today surges faster toward the sea, and scientists watch with keen interest.

The Antarctic community is self-regulating with the help of the Antarctic Treaty (AT), which came into force in 1961.

The AT is a very simple document, an international convention that emphasizes cooperation above all. When specific problems arise, the member nations, now numbering forty-five, add special agreements.

Twenty-seven of the forty-five AT nations are the actual decision makers.

There are two hundred special agreements now in place
to cover new management issues as they arise.

> While there are no airports per se, there are twenty Ant-
> arctic runways. Fifteen are gravel, sea ice, blue ice, or
> compacted snow; one runway is more than three kilo-
> meters in length. Two are of unknown length.

Expeditions are commonly referred to by their ship's
name:

> *Discovery*: 1901–1903, Robert Falcon Scott's first and only
> publicly funded expedition.

Nimrod: 1907–1909, Ernest Shackleton's first ship; on
this expedition he walked to within ninety miles of the
South Pole. ("Nimrod" means "mighty hunter.")

> *Terra Nova*: 1910–1912, Robert Falcon Scott's second, pri-
> vately funded, expedition; designed to get them to the
> geographic South Pole first.

Endurance: 1914–1916, sunk in the pack ice.

> The Intergovernmental Panel on Climate Change wins
> the Nobel Peace Prize, along with Al Gore, in 2007, for
> their efforts to "build up and disseminate knowledge
> about man-made climate change." In February 2007
> Dr. Susan Solomon, chair of the IPCC's Working Group
> I, gave the plenary address to the American Academy
> for the Advancement of Science annual meeting in San
> Francisco, and I attended with my daughter, Helena. (Dr.
> Solomon, a noted Antarctic scientist, also wrote a ter-
> rific account of Robert Falcon Scott's final trek to the
> South Pole, *The Coldest March*.) The whole Earth is being
> analyzed for change, she told us, and it has moved way
> beyond temperature to include ocean salinity, intensity

of storms, and wind patterns, among others. She cataloged changes afoot to a packed ballroom: global temperature rise of just over one degree in the past 150 years; a decrease in sea ice and land ice; highly dynamic glaciers—ice "speeding up" when ice shelves melted; more of Europe expected to become Mediterranean in climate; drying in the subtropics, wetter in the higher latitudes. Could this happen faster than it already is happening? We do not know, she said. The only continent without long-term baseline data is Antarctica: record keeping began in earnest in 1950.

Except for bars, gift shops, and post offices, no money changes hands in Antarctica. It is not a continent of shopkeepers and commerce. No passports are needed. It is a borderless, state-free wilderness.

Acknowledgments

Many brave people have set off for Antarctica to explore its icy wonder, yet few are known to us with the easy familiarity of drunken celebrities. Yet their stories are so much more engaging. Odd, isn't it? Who's in charge of all this, our culture, history, daily ration of stories? I don't have a chip on my shoulder about Famous People nor about Famous People We See in Museums and in BBC Documentaries, but I want to make it clear, no one makes it alone in Antarctica. Behind the heroes are legions of working-class men and women. Their marvelous stories of triumph in the face of adversity matter and should be much better represented in books, films, and museums.

Remembering the stories of the hardworking seamen who made Antarctic exploration possible has been the singular pursuit of Baden Norris. Baden worked with me over the course of many years and shared his stories and his wit and keen insights into Antarctican histories. As well, many sailors of yore have made this book possible: James Paton and

Frank Arthur Worsley, formidable explorers, recorded the days and nights of cold and ice that make books and films we enjoy today fact rather than armchair speculation. Both were keen observers of the natural world, and their diaries and letters bring to life an Antarctica we could not otherwise know. Worsley wrote books, and I recommend them to all who are interested in tales of the sea and exploration. He deserves to be elevated to a higher place in the pantheon of Antarctic and world heroes, for it was Worsley who masterminded and pulled off the greatest small boat journey known to us today. (Not to mention that in taking the time to tell the story well in all its vivid, salty, frozen detail, he shouts out to us from the grave that 1) stories matter more than, for instance, money, and 2) each day is an opportunity to show the world what you are made of.)

I offer gratitude to my colleagues at the University of Iowa: Mary, Cecile, Judy, Ed, Tom, Eric, Courtenay, Meredith, Sarah, Heal, Marilyn, Jo Ann, Patricia, Blake, Andy, Sue, Will, Maria, David, Cathy, Faith, and Paul. At the *Iowa Review* and the *Iowa Journal of Cultural Studies*, where we toiled to make collections of essays and stories, I doff my cap to David, Hugh, Megan, Anthony, Abe, and Kevin, as well as to my students Barrett, Christine, Mike, Jesse, Derek, and Gabe.

Lee at *Creative Nonfiction* selected my essay, "The Entire Earth and Sky," for anthology publication as second-place winner in a national competition for best essay. Other than a poster contest in third grade, it is my only contest victory and I will long cherish the memory of his phone call.

The poet and director of Iowa's International Writing Program, Christopher Merrill, encouraged my Fulbright application and later sent me an email that said simply, "courage." It came on a day when I felt little hope, and it made me stop feeling so forlorn about melting ice and simply write.

Fulbright New Zealand gave me money, and Gateway

Antarctica at the University of Canterbury gave me a room to write. Both offered limitless patience as well as key enthusiasm for this project. At Fulbright, I thank Jenny, Laurie, and Mele, as well as the Fellows Judy, George, Emily, Haley, Chris, and Tim, in particular. At Gateway, I thank Michelle, Bryan, Luke, Suzanna, Alan, and Paul.

Also in New Zealand, I thank Dave, Ana, Michael, Kerry, Roy, Maeve, Jack, Chris, Martin, and Stuart. At Antarctica New Zealand, I thank Lou Sanson for invaluable help.

In San Francisco, where I completed the manuscript, I got key encouragement from Susan and Michael, Ron, Eric, John, Michael C., Jamie, and most important, Ed.

Ladette, Kristen, Ann, Ray, and Sue at the University of Nebraska Press made the manuscript into a book, and they were always full of good cheer, insightful comments, and wit. I met Ladette at the Western Literature Association meeting, and she gave me her card and told me she would always be interested in reading. A terrific editor and humanist to whom I offer my unmitigated thanks.

From my Greenpeace days on the high seas, I thank Jim, Bob, Maggi, Bernadette, Ray, Ken, and Peter for keeping us all alive with sea smarts and good yarns.

My family has always supported me, and I have my father, Edwin, a great writer, as my model and guide. My mother, Barbara, and three sisters, Beth, Amy, and Jackie, are ready to offer kind words as spur. On the homefront, I am grateful for Ed. Also, Scott, for tireless support and faith, and Bob Halliday for his wit.

Finally, in New Zealand they call women like me "solo mums," a far more daring and attractive name than "single mother," which is my status in the United States. I want to thank my mother-pals, Erin, Ellen, Vivian, Linda, Jennifer, Sasha, and Julie, among many others, for cheering me on.

Photo Credits

Fig 1. Baden Norris in the Lyttelton Museum. *Author's collection.*

Fig. 2. James Paton and his two daughters (19xx.2.487). *Used courtesy of Canterbury Museum Archives, New Zealand.*

Fig. 3. The Terra Nova crew on parade (1980.243.2). *Used courtesy of Canterbury Museum Archives, New Zealand.*

Fig 4. Polar clothes. *Author's collection.*

Fig. 5. Deek's head. *Author's collection.*

Fig. 6. The ship Aurora. E. E. M. Joyce collection (1981.110.4). *Used courtesy of Canterbury Museum Archives, New Zealand.*

Fig. 7. The Aurora crew. *Used courtesy of Canterbury Museum Archives, New Zealand.*

Fig. 8. Red Cross certificate of Frank Arthur Worsley. MS539, item 45. *Used courtesy of Canterbury Museum Archives, New Zealand.*

Fig. 9. Terra Nova Antarctic expedition of 1910–1913: Tryggve Gran bathes. E. M. Harding collection (1967.126.1). *Used courtesy of Canterbury Museum Archives, New Zealand.*

Fig. 10. The Comet Scout primus stove. *Used courtesy of the Canterbury Museum Archives, New Zealand.*

Fig. 11. Polar Explorer toy box. *Author's collection.*

The Continent and Its History

A bucket of icy water down the neck checks the fiercest vomiter.
> —Frank Arthur Worsley, *Endurance*'s captain,
> on his cure for Antarctic seasickness.

Sometimes we are given our opportunities, and we take them and make something fine, and the story will live forever; and so we have our bodhisattva moment.
> —Kim Stanley Robinson, *Antarctica*

Antarctica is well worth reading about. It is not a common-place continent, but on the contrary is in all ways remarkable. The Antarctic continent is the fifth largest of the seven—the others being Africa, Asia, Australia, Europe, South America, and North America. If you want to fix its size, imagine the United States and Mexico combined. Antarctica is ranked eighth in geographic size of all the Earth's features.

Most of us have trouble calling to mind an overall image of Antarctica. This is because Antarctica gets edited off most world maps. The familiar mapped views of the world are Mercator projections, which maximize the area of midlatitude countries, thus making them appear larger than their geographic reality. Antarctica presents a pesky problem for mapmakers—as a circle it doesn't lend itself to being cut into one long, wide strip. The solution has been to leave it off maps entirely. So it was that the fifth-largest continent became a lacey fringe.

Lurking mysteriously off the map, Antarctic events invite

geographic context by scientists and news agencies. When an enormous iceberg broke off from the Antarctic Peninsula in 2002, its official name became B-22, a code describing location and time frame. The U.S. National Ice Center assigns these coded names, then monitors the bergs' journey northward. The agency is located outside of Washington DC, and most trackers have never seen an actual iceberg.

The gargantuan B-22 made news across the world—and caused editors and scientists to fish around for the words to describe its heft. The BBC described B-22 as nine times the size of Singapore, which presumably draws a picture for UK residents, all clear on their former colony's actual size. The Associated Press in the United States noted the berg rivaled the area of the state of Delaware. In Canada they offered Prince Edward Island as comparison. Reuters decided not to play that game, simply referring to the berg as "large." The game of scale is infectious for most, however. Want to imagine B-22 at its birth? Think of two Hawaiis or the Grand Duchy of Luxembourg.

B-22 had a short reign as a headline grabber. Within days, the British Antarctic Survey announced that satellites had captured the break up of the Larsen B Ice Shelf. The images of its demise, recorded by a passing camera miles above the Earth, made the *New York Times*'s front page, albeit below the fold. The Larsen B Ice Shelf weighed in at 500 billion tons, and filled Antarctica's Weddell Sea with miles of floes. What was the biggest floe, you ask? According to the *New Scientist*, it was about the size of Greater London.

Blue and white, vast flat plains of ice, wind-polished, sculpted, chewed. A clear blue sky. I look at images of Antarctica every day and have done so for nearly twenty years. While it's not precise to say humankind doesn't know very much about Antarctica's vast ice, it is accurate to say a lot of questions remain about how it works.

Scientists, as well as concerned observers such as myself, are particularly interested in what appear to be high degrees of variation of ice speed. The ice moves, from the high point of the South Pole outward to the continent's round-ish perimeter.

It used to be accepted fact that Antarctic glaciers were pretty stagnant. But this turned out to be false. They move all the time. They appear to be much more sensitive to other environmental factors than previously thought.

I peered at a slide of a helicopter buzzing along the face of the Barne Glacier, which extends into the Ross Sea at Cape Evans. I spent almost two months looking at the glacier, which from the sea looks like a blue and white stone cliff. The helicopter appears to be a tiny bug against its face. What we now know is that most of the Ross Ice Shelf, an ice formation the size of France, varies its speed in relation to the tides. The ice moves faster when the tide is high. The ice seems to respond to the moon's pull, like the ocean. The ice does not sit there, like a cap, on the Earth's base. The ice, one might say, has a mind of its own, its own agenda, its own flow.

I met a man named Luke who spent many weeks poking about $65,000 worth of probes into ice around the Ross Sea. No one had ever done this before in precisely the same way. He expressed hope that closer observation would show the many variants in the ice's speed and demonstrate exactly how sensitive it was.

Perhaps its mysterious absence from maps helps Antarctica retain its place in our cultural imagination. A twilight, a memoryscape, more fable than history, Antarctica's stories fuel artists' imaginations; perhaps artists feel the need to patch together stories left, like so much film, on the cutting room floor. History has always been unkind to the illiterate and those who fit into what may be called the poorer classes. Perhaps this explains why the stories poets, writers, and artists tell of place often diverge from the "facts" as found in books. Or that some books take on ideas of "science fiction" to explain a place few readers will ever see. When did the chronological sequence of events come to dictate so much about how we understand place and what it means to be human?

This is not meant as a small manifesto against conventional historians. A crowded field of heroes seems to appeal to no culture on Earth—we keep our lists of gods and saviors short and task specific. How God must laugh at this, our tiny minds at work!

How does this play out in Antarctica's brief human history? Men who actually achieved great insight and survived formidable conditions get dropped. I find some solace, however, in the realization that the men who accomplished great things weren't inspired to do so by the idea of living forever in some moldy book. They explored the unknown because the world was a real place to them, and real places are meant to be experienced not read about then forgotten while you make your daily wage. The 1902 Scottish National Antarctic Expedition comes to mind among the forgotten or little-known brought to life again by artists. Led by William Bruce, they wandered the Antarctic for two years and discovered and mapped Coats Land along the fierce Weddell Sea and were the first to use a motion picture camera in Antarctica—although Robert Falcon Scott's famed documentarian Herbert Ponting made the same claim later. The Bruce expedition also studied the effect of bagpipe music on penguins. To mark the one hundredth anniversary of Bruce's exploring, a variety of Scottish groups collaborated on a CD, *Music for the Scotia Centenary*. Included among the works are "The Piper and the Penguin," a tune played by Neil Barron and his Scottish Country Dance Band.

A friend recently suggested I give a listen to *The Songs of the Morning: A Musical Sketch* by G. S. Doorly. The *Morning* worked during the Heroic Age of Antarctic exploration, a supply ship run out of New Zealand by a fierce and brave crew, men who navigated the rough seas and icebergs to supply Scott when he first attempted to walk to the South Pole. The year was 1902 and Doorly served as third officer. He was also an accomplished pianist and parlor entertainer. He worked with the chief engineer, J. D. Morrison, to create songs, then performed during the ship's musical evenings. Seamen liked bawdy songs, real eyebrow raisers not designed for polite company, edgy material that helped to define their rough-hewn subculture. When you hear the lyrics and then bring to mind what comes out of iPods these days the idea that times change comes rather sonically to life. *Times change.* While I listened to the CD, I read the liner notes and stared out at the Pacific Ocean. A large blue freighter came chugging into the Golden Gate, loaded down with enormous metal containers. Everything that moves across the sea these days goes into these unromantic boxes, and periodically they spill off the deck in great storms and their contents entwine with the sea's currents and then small towns in Oregon find their beaches littered with yellow plastic ducks from China. Bath toys afloat in the Big Tub. On the repackaged version of the *Songs of the Morning*, all of Doorly's adult male descendants sing in the chorus.

Finn Ronne was a noted American midcentury Antarctic explorer, and his daughter Karen Ronne recorded an Antarctic love song, "Antarctic Dreams"; her grandfather went south with Roald Amundsen, the first man to the South Pole; Finn traveled with Byrd, then set off on his own expedition to the Antarctic Peninsula. Finn brought his wife, and another colleague brought along his wife as well, and these two became the first women to winter in Antarctica. Largely forgotten today, Jennie Darlington wrote a book about this first-women

adventure, *My Antarctic Honeymoon*. In it she describes the life
of an Antarctic wife, complete with discussions of Antarctic histories and how many lipsticks she packed to last the
year. Once I made it known to my friends that I was seeking all musical references to Antarctica, CDs seemed to flow
through the mail to me, including one from New Jersey fea-
turing the local metal band Ironia who found inspiration
in Ernest Shackleton and the ship *Endurance*. The lyrics of
"Shackleton Perseveres" have been described as matching the
story of the *Endurance*, which was trapped in Antarctica's ice
and crushed, leaving her twenty-eight-man crew to fend for
themselves over three seasons before they could seek help
at the whaling station on South Georgia. The song includes
these words, "'Well, should we just lie down and die?' he cried,
'No! We'll set sail toward South Georgia isle!'"

Each expedition pushed or developed the idea of an indigenous Antarctican culture. At McMurdo, the largest base in
Antarctica and run by the U.S. National Science Foundation,
workers created an ongoing music festival, Icestock. Icestock
apparently suffers in terms of musicality—dry air and cold
warp instruments—but still each New Year's Day musicians
gather and play whatever style of music appeals. It makes for
a messy, impromptu feel and perhaps best reflects the experience of living in Antarctica, where mood and weather fluc-
tuate at alarming rates. Cultural nadir, movements, clusters
of artists with group names and group impact, require a certain synchronicity of time, money, political mood, and dare
I say, barometric pressure. Not unlike polar explorers. Kin,
perhaps, explorers in search of the unknown, living on the
fringe of proper society.

The classic Antarctic symphony, Ralph Vaughn Williams's
Sinfonia Antartica began its life as the score for the 1949 film
Scott of the Antarctic. In the film, less than half of the original

score is heard, and Vaughn Williams later took the music
and reworked it into his *Sinfonia*.

At the heart of my inquiry into the continent and its histories
lies a fascination with how we understand a remote, unin-
habitable place through stories. This comment sounds rather
ghostlike to my ear, almost menacing, in the way academ-
ics writing about books scare the pants off me, using words
like "elide" or talking about how a certain French philosopher offered a particular "lens" for understanding and har-
nessing ideas presented in a certain novel. (When I first published *The Entire Earth and Sky* as an essay, the editor wrote
that it was all about "death." Balderdash! It is about walking on a beach and how when we walk we record the scene
and the feelings with each piece of our bodies, it's about how
throwing our bodies at a landscape helps us to dissolve into a
home environment—minerals and water being the building
blocks of humanity as well as boulder-covered shores.) My
interest rose from the ether of considering the "little known"
stories—not stories that are little known because they are
essentially dull, but stories that perish because their tellers
perhaps are illiterate, or are too busy doing other things to
write them down. Walt Whitman in his later years never left
his room, spent all of his time writing things down. Annie
Dillard writes about this in a book about the writing life, and
how we choose our subjects as writers for reasons that are
hard to articulate. So the world is immersed in the stories
of people like myself, those inclined to wander outside and
equally inclined to scribble down what they see and then find
a way to force their account onto various shelves in sundry
libraries and digital book emporiums.

Because I keep a notebook and jot down my observations,
and because I sailed in Antarctica as crew not captain or
leader, I feel a particular kinship to the simple seamen who

recorded their adventures through letters and diaries. (The expedition leaders also bear less interest to me because they wrote their books out of duty and desire to make money, usually. Books by polar explorers were bestsellers in the early part of the twentieth century, and they were rushed off the press to an eager public. These books were an important part of funding the entire endeavor, as were the photos and moving pictures shot and later turned into lantern slide shows and cinema offerings.)

Even today, as more than thirty-seven thousand tourists head south each summer to get a look, the main way people learn about Antarctica, of course, remains books like this one. I follow the field and it seems more than two dozen come out each year, not counting the highly specialized scientific treatises, each with its own audience of six. If you add those books, the number of Antarctic books published annually is about 836.

One thing that may strike the reader of these stories is just this: How simple acts of survival—making a meal of tea and hot porridge, getting into a sleeping bag, walking—can become singular essays, or indeed whole chapters. There is also an Antarctican joke about some of the more recent offerings, now that Antarctica is really not a place where one goes under peril of death. *If the story had happened anywhere else, it would be of no interest whatsoever.* But set it in Antarctica and, well, say no more. For instance, a man falls and breaks his leg. Thousands of men do this each summer while attempting to paint their own homes, stretching from unbalanced ladders. "Fool!" we say, after we call in to wish him our best. If the same man fell in Antarctica while climbing on the ice-covered roof of a hut, we would stand at attention. How did the man recover? What was the man thinking as he slid the five or six feet to the ground? Were there any penguins around while he fell?

First-person accounts reflect our interest in hearing news of the battle from the frontlines. For many decades, indeed for most of the twentieth century, Antarctic books focused on the keen sense of camaraderie, the brave and bold, the quest for knowledge to such an extreme that one was *willing to die*. Men willing to die to find out how penguins reproduced occupy a central part of the classic book of Antarctic exploration, *The Worst Journey in the World*. This book stands out from all others because more than any other quality, it honestly considers the absurdity of these pursuits. The book's author, Apsley Cherry-Garrard, spent most of his post-Antarctic life depressed and living on an estate in the English countryside. If you read his work carefully, you can see how ill-suited modern culture is to understanding the motivations of these men who set out for the ice. Cherry, as he was known, argues that people could not appreciate the grace and simple courage that lay behind the heroic face, like some hideous mask, hung on these men.

I don't know if Cherry would enjoy the modern first-person Antarctic narrative, which often does little to advance the idea of gracious living on the ice. Among the hundreds of people I interviewed when researching this book was the explorer George Lowe. Lowe was Edmund Hillary's climbing buddy, scaled Everest with him on the triumphant ascent, then crossed Antarctica over land with the British explorer Vivian "Bunny" Fuchs, as Hillary rolled from the other side of the continent, the parties to meet at the South Pole. It would be the first overland crossing of the continent.

Lowe regularly attends meetings as an honored guest— seated alongside the likes of Neil Armstrong, the first man to walk on the moon. When Lowe and I met for lunch, he told me the first question most people asked was how they went to the toilet during the Antarctic crossing. Then he proceeded to describe the drill: two men in a tent, swapping jobs day to day, one man digging the toilet hole in the ice and snow, taking turns using it, covering the hole. Funny, as he narrated the drill, my mind wandered and I tried to recall if this detail of Antarctic life had ever been of interest to me. It was, in fact, exactly what one would imagine.

What I wanted to know was, what did Lowe do all day when they drove their Sno-cats 1,988 miles (3200 km) across the ice? Lowe's vehicle served as the anchor behind the leader's— that is, if Fuchs went down a crevasse, Lowe's, tethered to it, would halt its plunge into the abyss. At least that was the theory. Lowe quickly responded, "I read *War and Peace*. The same book I read when we climbed Everest." When I asked why *War and Peace*, Lowe replied it was *a good book one never tired of.*

At any rate, the newish first-person accounts reveal all sorts of degenerate, dark qualities of modern Antarctic life—it's like a play on words, the groups of huts where they live are called *bases*. People drink alcohol to excess, often have sex with relative strangers—many of these couples have loving partners awaiting them at home—and spend their free time in pathetic discos they create in the base bar.

I read these modern accounts with some delight. So you can imagine my surprise and good cheer when I found myself seated at a dinner in New Zealand next to a relation of one recent Antarctican memoirist. The memoir, written by an Australian woman who cooked at a remote South African Antarctic base, covered the usual ground, and offered *People* magazine–style reportage on her affair with a married American scientist. The man who was my dinner companion was this man's brother; the author had become his sister-in-law. He shook his head while admitting this: "My mother was mortified."

It is a far cry from the accounts of the early explorers, who brought a scholarly, pious, and gentlemanly vernacular to Antarctic life. Because Antarctica appears in books and films defined by its superlatives—highest, driest, coldest—the embedded idea seems to be that anything people do there by association also falls into the superlative realm.

You may wonder why, at the turn of the twentieth century, so many people started trying to break through the Antarctic's icy boundaries. The main motivator, of course, was colonialism. People hoped to find coal, gold, and other saleable minerals there. People hoped to expand their realm. In addition, small but key innovations had evolved in cold weather travel, one of which was a tiny stove called a Primus. This offered a low-fuel means of heating food and melting ice fast. Men could venture into the unknown with a reasonable chance of making it far afield and back without freezing to death because of the Primus. I have heard this little stove, which fits inside a cocoa tin, described as the key to unlocking the Antarctic continent.

People also couldn't bear the idea of a completely unknown place. Antarctica had all sorts of wild theories suggested about it—chief among them that its ice yielded to a great hole at the geographic South Pole, a portal into a series of worlds within our world, stacked together like one of those Russian dolls. While this notion might strike some as far-fetched it had strong advocates and national funding—an expedition funded by the U.S. government to seek answers to this pressing question set sail in the late 1830s.

Most historians seem content to point to London, and the decree by the Royal Geographic Society in 1895 that the time had come to figure out what was down there once and for all. And so as the new century dawned, the final, thickly curtained portion of the Earth's surface would begin to reveal itself. People would follow the expeditions to Antarctica the way a later generation would follow the moon race. As a student of these stories, I can attest that you will find few other places where the tales are consistently as harrowing, gritty, and revelatory.

The now little-known Antarctic explorer Frank Arthur Worsley came into my life in 1988. By this time, he had been dead for forty-five years. In addition to his books, copies of his handwritten diaries, and many news accounts of his life, over the years I have collected his obituaries, published and aired around the world.

From the esteemed journal *Nature*, a narrative of his life, with significant opinion: "Worsley was a man of action, always on the move and extremely alert, both mentally and physically. . . . He was not a man of science in the strict sense of the word, but he was a born naturalist and observer, as the logs he kept on his cruises bear out. . . . It was as a navigator, however, that he stood supreme, and there is nothing finer than his piloting of the *James Caird* to South Georgia, an island not more than a speck on the wide South Atlantic Ocean."

Worsley was master of Shackleton's ship *Endurance* for the 1914–1917 Imperial Trans-Antarctic Expedition. The *Endurance*, Shackleton's second Antarctic command, entered the pack ice in the Weddell Sea late in 1914, worked its way in adverse weather southward, where they discovered the Caird Coast in Coats Land. Trapped in ice, the ship was crushed in October 1915. The twenty-eight-man crew then moved onto the ice, surviving in makeshift camps prone to breaking up under their feet, and patrolled by hungry orcas looking for a meal. They drifted northward, until they set sail in their three small lifeboats, arriving at the sub-Antarctic island called Elephant after six days. On this grim rock, they hatched plans to send one boat off for help—there being no radio contact with the outside world from Antarctica in those days. Worsley then navigated a twenty-two-foot lifeboat, named *James Caird*, on an epic journey from Elephant Island to South Georgia.

Worsley wrote of this small-boat adventure in a slender volume titled *Shackleton's Boat Journey*. He also included the story in his longer book about the expedition, *Endurance*. It was unusual for a sea captain on an Antarctic ship to become a full-time writer, but this was Worsley's path. He supported himself and his wife, according to his biographer John Thomson, for the last decades of his life, with his writing.

But something else was going on here as well, writing and publishing the same adventure story twice. Frank Worsley had another agenda, I believe. Much of his writing captured the years during which he had come of age as a mariner, 1895–1922, which precisely coincede with what historians now call the Heroic Age of Antarctic Exploration.

These years were akin to a later generation's face for the Moon: Innovation, jealousy, military might, fuel, grudges, training, avarice, gossip, food, clothing, leadership, envy, and pure luck. It was that rare moment in human history when the people with the right balance of all of the above would win a prize of incomparable, yet wholly unquantifiable, value. Because the poles were not simply about getting there, they were all about getting there first.

The South Pole quest began in earnest in November 1901, when a purpose-built Antarctic expedition ship named *Discovery* sailed into Lyttelton, Frank Arthur Worsley's home port, which skirted the interior of a partially submerged, long-extinct volcano, a stunning, protected anchorage rising from deep turquoise waters of the far South Pacific.

Robert Falcon Scott stands in direct contrast to Worsley, and it is an interesting comparison. Perhaps the most studied, lauded, and reviled explorer of all time, Scott turned out to be a woeful leader in stressful times, adhering to protocol and the letter of British naval operations even when in *terra incognita*.

However, these facts of Scott's story serve to discredit his efforts, and it is inaccurate to contribute to so easy a dismissal. Surely a man of such narrow views and thin character could not have imagined the need to explore the unknown. Surely beyond the facts of his life as told we can look at the facts of his existence in Antarctica. Here is a man who walked not once, but twice in the direction of the South Pole. The second time, he made it there. He almost made it back. No one has ever done what Scott and his men pulled off—walking, without dogs, and pulling heavy sledges across hundreds of miles of Antarctic ice. This walk began in October. They trudged across crevasse-laced ice and arrived at the South Pole in January. Try to imagine their fortitude.

To this day, Scott's memory hovers like a huge airship over Antarctic histories. His widow and son were celebrities throughout their lives. An entire industry of remembering sprang from his failed endeavor. At Cambridge University, the most important academic center for polar histories, you wander the stacks of the Scott Polar Research Institute. "I may be some time," words uttered by his colleague, Laurence Titus Oates, before wandering off to a cold Antarctic death, were memorized by school children across Britain's vast commonwealth. Museums telling early twentieth-century histories have rafts of calendars, cards, posters, and other printed materials to choose from; he died what many now agree was a fool's death, yet his death was and is examined by scores, in dozens of books, a feature film, and museum displays around the world. Scott's legacy evolves, holding its own as iconic story of Antarctica, harrowing polar exploration, bravery, tragedy, and hubris. All these things and then this, Scott was a man who wanted to walk to the South Pole. There are not many men who feel this desire. Desire or idea then fantasy or list making then landscape or the march across the white abyss. The tonic sense of finally and at long last being home.

Scott's apocalyptic legend stomps across all stories of his day, indeed across the first hundred years of South Polar exploration. When his time as an Antarctic explorer falls under scrutiny—each choice becomes weighted in a manner that gives me pause. Where to begin with their mistakes? First, Scott and his men did not know how to ski when they went to Antarctica. On their second trip, they brought along a Norwegian ski expert, Tryggve Gran. (Gran went on to have a stellar career in aviation, marred in the end, however, by his support of Hermann Goering.) Perhaps more importantly, a man's class and character (one and the same in England in those days) ranked higher than physical strengths. Thus, Scott set off for the South Pole on his second attempt with one man who had been shot in the leg while in the army (Lawrence Oates), one man who had suffered from tuberculosis (Edward Wilson), two men who were both strong and fit (Edgar Evans and Henry Bowers), and himself, by then in his early forties, with little training in manhauling sledges weighing more than three hundred pounds across the ice.

If you close your eyes for a moment, and imagine these five men manhauling towards the Pole, it may be difficult to simply dismiss them as fools. You might be inclined to see them as consummately brave, brave in a manner we rarely see in our well-equipped world of polar travel.

They wore Burberry anoraks, made of tightly woven cotton. They had fur and wool to keep them warm, but their outer layer, the final shield against the coldest, strongest, most howling winds on the planet, were simple cotton coats. I once held one of these beige jackets, brushed the stiff cotton against my cheek, smelled the strange scent of old fabric. Cotton. I don't know about you, but something in this detail makes Scott's expeditions and all of the contemporaries seem marvelous. Cold cannot be imagined.

Landscape. Fantasy. Desire.

How we place ourselves in a landscape. How we tell the story of a continent covered in ice. How we make sense of why it exists in the first place, and more importantly, *what are we going to do there?*

New Zealand houses more Antarctic museums than any other country in the world. In Christchurch, a city of 350,000 on the South Island, there are three museums within a thirty-minute drive of one another. Depending on how you count, more could be added to that list. If history is written by the winners, culture belongs to those who possess objects and deploy them selectively to illuminate stories. Storytelling sets us free while slipping on the manacles. Language offers a technology for placing ourselves into a landscape. What is the syntax of Antarctica?

The Greatest Antarctic Story of All Time (A Note)

It was late in April; the southern winter was upon us. Daily, while watching for the sun, I went up the 150-foot rock to the north of the camp to watch the extent and movement of the ice starting to drift past the island on the northeast current. Broken-up floes and streams of ice—scouts and skirmishes of the vanguard of the Great White Fleet— had already appeared. Borne each year from their icy fastnesses in the Antarctic by the broad stream that pours up through Bransfield Strait, they spread out in the winter through spillways of the South Shetlands, enveloping Clarence and Elephant Islands for weeks at a time.

— Frank Arthur Worsley,
from Shackleton's Boat Journey

When Frank Arthur Worsley picked up the chronometer on Easter Monday, 1916, the fate of twenty-eight men lay in his skill as a navigator. Luckily for the men of Ernest Shackleton's *Endurance* expedition, Worsley was a brilliant navigator. And he was about to steer a course that would become one of the greatest feats of small boat navigation known to man.

Shortly after breakfast on that cold Antarctic morning, the sun obliged Worsley, and he was offered a clear enough horizon to get a sight for rating his chronometer. This device, the last in working order of the twenty-four with which the *Endurance* had set out on December 5, 1914, allowed him to begin calculating the longitudinal path ahead.

The six men had an inauspicious beginning, overballasting their cramped, converted lifeboat—called *James Caird* after a generous expedition donor—which caused "slowness, stiffness, and jerky motion," according to Worsley. Worsley had argued with Shackleton that a heavy boat would be a wet boat, but Shackleton, worried about underballasting, took other counsel.

Worsley, of course, was right. Close to thirty years as a Pacific sailor and ship's master had built an understanding and instinct about the sea that surpassed any other of the *Endurance*'s crew. The boat was pounded by seas, and the men and all their gear were soaked relentlessly by freezing seawater. The other two lifeboats were used to ferry their supplies, including Worsley's sextant and navigation books. Then it was time to leave. Their fate had always been linked inextricably to Worsley's skill as a navigator; now, however, this was brought into sharp focus. His task was to move the *Caird* through close to eight hundred miles of howling, early winter, polar seas to the whaling station at South Georgia. How does one put into words the meaning of this boat launch? It was, so emphatically, their last hope. Frank Worsley was forty-three years old. The New Zealander had been at sea since the age of fifteen. He has been described as an exceptionally tough and able seaman, with an equal measure of courage, strength, and spirit of adventure. He would soon prove to them that he was, to use a modern cliché, *the man*.

It was Frank Worsley's small book, *Shackleton's Boat Journey*, that hooked me on the idea of "little known" Antarctic stories. That is to say, Worsley is relatively unknown (do most people know his feat as they know Bligh's?) and has only recently and rarely (the last fifteen years) been elevated to museum-quality status. Yet when he died in 1943, his obituary appeared in newspapers and magazines all over the world. Then, nothing. It was his precipitous drop from the historical radar that motivated me as I recorded others' stories of Antarctic exploration. I was not looking for stories as bold or urgent or dire—they are, actually, few and far between in these times, when the number 1 cause of death in Antarctica is industrial accidents.

Antarctic stories are linked by place, a place that serves as lure and obsession for a small percentage of those who go there. Worsley, I believe, felt this, and understood it as part of his need to remain peripatetic throughout his lush adventures. In the end, these are stories of people who seek, in a variety of manners, the unknown. The lines from Eliot, "We shall not cease from exploration / And the end of all our exploring / Will be to arrive where we started / And know the place for the first time," are so widely deployed as epigraph I feel the need to cast our eyes on them here. Why do they hold so much meaning for Antarcticans? I think the answer is clear: Antarctica offers us a lens on deep time in its striking geomorphologies and a mirror for our deepest nomadic longings in its border-free, wide-open spaces. We look up, stretching neck back, and breathe deeply the entire Earth and sky.

You can read snow surfaces, provided the light's good. Like any scrawled out language. You could see crevasses, invariably a different texture from the rest of the white, wide ice. Imagine flying out to sea, nothing else behind you as reference—no two flights the same, all below a code, glyphs, a language describing the current reality of ice.

Field Notes

One

I can take society well enough, so long as I keep my rubber gloves on. Although lately, I have to say I keep feeling the irrepressible urge to cut off my ear and catch the next train to Antarctica.

—J. D. Salinger

Lyttelton, New Zealand, to Cape Evans, Antarctica

I sailed to Antarctica with a group of people who wanted to save the world. The world, in this case, meant Antarctica's ice-shrouded 5.4-million-square miles, a crystalline fortress separated from the known or temperate world by a ring of howling, fierce ocean. There is nothing more alone in this world than Antarctica. Once the center of a great southern supercontinent, it became a fragment, drifting south to the pole, where the seas and winds conspired to seal it in a horrible cold. Ice took over, offering a jumble of milk-stained cliffs and green glassware. When the sun shines the whole place lights up better than the Emerald City, and it is the most beautiful place on Earth.

I was young then and did not realize there remained places not only called the unknown, but actual unknown regions of Earth—unseen, untouched, unmapped, places no one had yet named or even set eyes on. In Antarctica, a requirement of entry is leaving your eyes behind after you have a new pair installed. Then you get the chance to see the world again as though for the first time, and even your own home and mother make you stop and revel in wonder. *My God*, you find yourself saying, *I love the smell of rain on hot concrete.* Transformation is a great idea as long as you don't think about it too much.

Our ship was a donated oceangoing tug, designed to pull large freighters to and from port; Dutch-built with enormous Smit-Man engines, most of her career had been spent working coastal Maryland for the pilots' association. (Coincidentally about forty miles from where I grew up outside of Washington DC.) We had ample engine power but lacked a hull wholly reinforced for ice. What this gained in narrative color, it lost in mind-numbing terror. (Later, when it was too late and we were already at sea deep in the Antarctic, one old salt noted she was a very dangerous ship for ice, neither designed nor modified to deal with hits from rock-hard ice. Later still, when Antarcticans learned I traveled on this old ship, my choice to do so came to be considered—falsely I might add—"brave.") Fitted with brass and polished, dark wood, about thirty years old, Greenpeace sailed her south to scrutinize polar research stations and create outrage about Antarctic mining schemes being hashed out at closed-door international meetings.

I recall cruising through the long tunnel separating Lyttelton—a colonial port town established in the mid-nineteenth century, later home and workplace for dozens of polar explorers and their crews—from the larger metropolitan area of Christchurch, New Zealand, on a hot, bright January morning, and seeing our ship tied up at the quayside, flanked by Nedlloyd freighters and coastal supply ships, and in contrast to them our ship appeared pitifully small, like a black-and-ocher bath toy festooned with a rainbow, a hopeful little tub. The cab driver wanted to know why I was going to the quayside. I told him we were heading to Antarctica to save the world, something I had come to enjoy telling people, to which he looked aghast in the rearview mirror, then asked me if I believed in God. Do you know, he began, that a ship sank down there only two years ago? I knew the ship he was talking about, and it scared me in a profound way; yet a growing urgency to be in Antarctica overshadowed fear. As I paid the driver, he looked at me and said, "Really, God bless you."

Many Antarctic stories begin with a bright moment of realization or even a dream—illustrating the narrator's ineluctable destiny as a polar explorer. My story begins with this scene: a Greenpeace press kit sliding off my desk one morning in Melbourne, Australia. Antarctica smiled at me from the cascade of photos; an ice-shrouded steaming volcano, gleaming blue ice, tiny red-eyed penguins, a slick black whale fin. Under threat! The press release screamed. The images lodged in my brain but something else happened as well, I cannot say what it was exactly, but I knew I would go south. This certainty offered a feeling akin to that of arriving home on a cool, autumn afternoon, as the sun angles lower in the sky, and a warm yellow lamp shines hopefully in the front window. It is a feeling that has never left me, and comes to me each time I read or write the word *Antarctica*.

I began reading stories about Antarctica that night as I rode home across the Yarra River on one of Melbourne's famed wooden trams. Small girls wearing straw boaters and navy coats filled the tram. I had recently moved across the world from Sarasota, Florida, and found work at Melbourne's afternoon daily newspaper, settling down with my longtime beau. This man, it turned out, wooed many, from the features editor at a competing newspaper to a former beauty queen from Texas. I spent most evenings sitting on the kitchen counter, tapping my fingers on the green, glitter-flecked Formi-

ca and eating popcorn; by day I wrote about food and chefs
and sampled whitebait omelets, Champagne, Mongolian
barbecue, and sobbed in the toilet stall. Antarctica offered
me a way out.

So I called Greenpeace's London office and talked to a
man named Martin who told me I must interview with the
crew, at present in New Zealand preparing for Antarctica.
"By the way," he added, "there is a New Zealand story here,
too. We're finally putting what's left of the *Rainbow Warrior*
down as a diving reef. Big memorial offshore to the ship,
her mission, and the man the French government killed." A
week later, I got on a plane for the three-hour flight to Auckland and arrived at midnight, from where I joined the Greenpeace yacht *Vega* and sailed north, at midmorning entering
stunningly beautiful Matauri Bay, on New Zealand's eastern
coast. Helicopters swooped overhead. Small cabin cruisers
and bright-colored yachts formed a white-and-silver flotil-
la of mourning. What was left of the *Rainbow Warrior* slowly sank to the bottom as a diving reef, while her crew stood
in an inflatable boat watching surging air bubbles roil the
surface. Two years earlier, French navy divers set charges on
the *Rainbow Warrior*'s hull and blasted the ship in Auckland
harbor, killing one of her crew; while Pacific island nations,
Greenpeace, and others had engaged in a long, often violent fight over French nuclear testing in the South Pacific,
the French response stunned the world.

After the ceremony, we set up camp on a dark beach illuminated by a pyre-like bonfire and a dense pack of stars overhead.
Whiskey bottles passed around, someone played a drum; it
shimmered, a tribal, strange, hippies-on-the-high-seas aesthetic and exactly what I anticipated. And that was how I
wrote the story when I returned home to pack my bags for
Antarctica, having secured a spot on the thirty-two-mem-
ber crew.

Lyttelton, a deep-water port built within a slowly eroding, 11-million-year-old volcano on New Zealand's east coast, tells a story of Antarctic embarkation—the wonder, thrill, mystery—of the last, great terrestrial explorations, a role dictated by its close geographic proximity, a town where the great explorers lived and worked and worshiped God before they set sail.

Eight women sailed on our ship, two cooks, one of the mates, an able-bodied seaman, a zoologist, a geologist, the doctor, and me; I quickly fell in with third mate Bernadette, of County Wexford, Ireland, and Maggie of New York's Hudson Valley, who was a seaman and boat driver—Maggie dropped out of college and sailed off with Greenpeace because of the whale issue, she explained, elaborating that the Japanese and others needed to stop killing and eating them. Bernadette was a professional ship's mate and had worked for Shell moving tankers across the North Pacific. This low-paying Greenpeace stint was an effort, she explained, to get back her karmic balance.

During the day, people worked with little rest; huge mesh bags of carrots coming on board, yellow paint scraped and replaced by white paint, stores counted, arranged, balanced; everything had to balance in the hold. I read books about polar exploration and tried to stay out of the way. At night, the sailors played pool at the British Hotel, a grotty, wharfside pub, and I followed along; one night some sailors from another ship got into a fistfight and one was stabbed with a screwdriver, a sight even the seasoned sailors noted as gruesome. The injured man was helped up steep concrete steps to a medic, then they mopped up the floor with sudsy water, circles of white, gray, red, pink. Then the crack of pool balls filled the air, impassive faces returned, a local beer called Tui was poured all around.

Greenpeace exuded rock-band cool, complete with group-

Baden Norris, *Antarctic curator, historian, and explorer, sitting on a bench taken from the* Terra Nova *in the Lyttelton Museum Polar Gallery.*

ies—women and men eager to meet the heroes off to fight for Antarctica—and they waited among the inflated, black-and-white plastic penguins, vivid photos of whales breeching, dangling crystals refracting so many tiny rainbows, waiting for someone to talk to them; they usually mistakenly assumed I had an active role in this scheme to save the world, too, and gave me a certain look of admiration. So I fled the docks for the musty calm of the Lyttelton Historical Society's museum, upstairs to the eccentric Polar Gallery.

While I stood there in the quiet, dim light one afternoon, gazing at a badly preserved emperor penguin, a calm, resonant voice began, "This penguin was brought back by a local sailor named James Paton; penguin décor was part of Lyttelton in the early twentieth century. Many had such stuffed

Antarctic souvenirs in their entryways," I turned and saw a man with bright blue eyes and silver hair; he wore a pressed shirt and his face was sculptural in its wrinkles. I introduced myself as a writer going south with Greenpeace and extended my hand.

He said, "I'm Baden Norris, Antarctic curator here and at the Canterbury Museum. I was just off to make some tea. Do you want a cup?"

While Baden made tea, I recounted our Antarctic agenda, covering four months, weather and ice permitting. Baden knew of us, polar ships in Lyttelton being well publicized. People still came from all over the South Island to get a look at them.

"Our first stop will be Cape Evans," I began, but Baden interrupted me: "Well, it's good we met then," he said. "I have spent some time at Cape Evans, beginning in the early 1960s. You will come to see how your own story begins to mirror the story of Lyttelton itself."

What, I wondered, did that mean?

"You'll see," he said. "Want some biscuits?"

And so he began untangling Lyttelton's Antarctic ties for me, ties evident even in the facts of his own Lyttelton roots— born in a wharfside hospital and reared surrounded by sailors' tales of sea, ships, and polar exploration—his grandparents once owned a farm further around the harbor, land later sold and made into a large quay for today's oceangoing freighters.

"When the First World War ended, Lyttelton became home to more Antarctic explorers than any other place on Earth. They worked together on the docks, men from all the great expeditions of the Heroic Age," Baden recounted, men whose stories animated the town's pubs and drawing rooms.

He paused a moment and said, "And I had the privilege of meeting many of them—including a man from Shackleton's famous boat journey—my father once took me to visit Harry McNeish." McNeish famously sailed as ship's carpenter with Ernest Shackleton on the *Endurance* expedition of 1914–1917. You don't have to read too far into *Endurance*'s story to find McNeish, the Antarctic's most famous mutineer. (McNeish argued that once the *Endurance* sank, the crew was not obligated to accept Shackleton's leadership, because their contracts were to follow orders at sea, not when living on the ice.)

While McNeish famously stood in opposition to Shackleton at times, the carpenter's fame is also linked to his companion, a male cat named Mrs. Chippy. Mrs. Chippy had to be shot when they abandoned ship, to spare her the fate of dogs ripping her to pieces on the ice. (Shackleton never forgot how McNeish refused his leadership and denied the carpenter the prestigious Polar Medal bestowed by the king on crewmates when they returned to London.) McNeish later emigrated to New Zealand, where he became an immediate wharfside celebrity; New Zealanders have always lauded Antarctic explorers beyond the recognition offered by the rest of the world. Baden's father had been a sailor, and when he heard the McNeish was dying, they traveled by ferry to pay their respects to him in Wellington. Baden was barely school age. Wharf workers in Wellington rallied to care for McNeish, Baden said. "I recall his small, dark room . . . McNeish gestured to us . . . come to his bedside," Baden said. "I was terrified. My father held my hand. He wanted us to honor McNeish, a hardworking ship's carpenter who had survived Antarctica's most dramatic shipwreck. McNeish wanted to tell us something. He could barely raise his head from the pillow, and leaned his face close to mine. In a hoarse whisper he said, 'Shackleton killed my cat.'"

Baden and I often met after that in the Lyttelton Museum, where I would read old newspapers from the days of Shackleton and Scott while he tinkered and explained what it was like to grow up in Lyttelton, a town we came to call the "Cape Canaveral of Antarctic exploration"—I liked the analogy with *The Right Stuff*, a bunch of brave nobodies shot out into the stratosphere, pushing the edge of the envelope, some to become legendary, some to slip into the dim world of the forgotten. All still brave. All still had done it.

Baden went to sea at fifteen, and Mortimer "Jack" McCarthy, an Irishman from Kinsale, then a Lyttelton resident, was among his crewmates. McCarthy had sailed with Robert Falcon Scott's *Terra Nova* expedition of 1910, part of the crew that challenged ferocious seas to get Scott safely on his way to the South Pole.

Baden showed me a fine photograph of McCarthy, a tall man with a handlebar moustache and a pipe, standing at a ship's wheel, wind blowing the sea to great crests not an arm length from where he stood. McCarthy had been a kind man with the empathy to help young sailors' stave off homesickness—through lively stories of his great Antarctic adventures. As a boy, Baden had played with McCarthy's sons in the streets of Lyttelton. One was named Tim. Many years later, Baden discovered that McCarthy's brother, Tim, had sailed to the Antarctic with Shackleton and Worsley aboard *Endurance*. A strong and good-natured man, Tim was among the six who made Worsley's brilliant small boat journey from Elephant Island to South Georgia. The Tim we meet in books about the *Endurance* is a tough North Sea fisherman, imbued with grace and wit and a single-minded determination to not only survive, but to do so with good cheer. Like most of the *Endurance*'s crew, Tim returned from three seasons trapped in Antarctica and enlisted immediately in World War I. He would die within months of his return, shot dead at a gunnery post while at sea with the British Navy. This fact was almost too much for me to bear.

Jack McCarthy had been the first man to sight the Norwegian explorer Roald Amundsen's ship, the *Fram*, in the Bay of Whales. While Amundsen had announced his intent to explore and locate the South Pole, the fact of another ship in remote Antarctic waters jarred *Terra Nova*'s crew. The British had a proprietary sense of Antarctica. Some of the *Terra Nova*'s seamen wanted to fight it out with the Norwegians then and there, McCarthy later told the boys. But the officers would have none of that, so they returned to Cape Evans to leave word for Scott: The race to the South Pole was on.

Once the *Greenpeace* sailed, with Baden and about a hundred others waving good-bye from the quayside, we quickly hit gale-force-eight seas. The ship's bucking and jerking terrified me. I tried to fill my mind with Antarctic stories, as a stay against fear. I read how in 1839 the Englishman James Clark Ross arrived in the South Pacific, determined to answer questions of what, exactly, the Antarctic was: Ice? Land? Gold?

In his possession was a hundred-page instruction book from the Royal Geographic Society, a detailed account of every object of inquiry that learned body could devise.

In 1841 Ross navigated his two ships, *Erebus* and *Terror*, southward, threading them through pack ice. The men described the belching flame and smoke of the world's southernmost active volcano, which they named Erebus after their ship. Ross compared the great ice shelf to the White Cliffs of Dover.

Ross's expeditions also began the long and fabled Antarctic tradition of wild parties and inventive entertainments. Alan Gurney, in *The Race to the White Continent*, writes, "The player of female roles in Arctic theatricals had metamorphosed into one of the Royal Navy's most handsome and one of its most scientific officers. Beginning in 1818, the 37-year-old Ross had spent eight winters and fifteen summers explor-

ing the Arctic." When *Terror* and *Erebus* spent New Year's Eve
in the Ross Sea, the men carved a pub from thick sea ice and
celebrated, sculpting a dance floor and ice chairs for Ross
and his officers. A flag flew above all these hijinks, the same
flag that flew over the North Magnetic Pole. It announced,
"Pilgrim of the Ocean," and on the other side, "The Pioneers
of Science."

Ross, an enthusiastic naturalist, had included among his
crew twenty-one-year-old Joseph Hooker, a naturalist, as
the sole nonmilitary man on board. (Hooker's methods for
prying lichens out of icy sub-Antarctic island rocks made a
keen impression on me: Hooker records sitting on lichens,
using his rear end to thaw the area sufficiently, allowing for
the lichens' collection as specimens.) Ross's Antarctic discoveries are considered among the most remarkable of the
nineteenth century. His reports of the Antarctic, and his
discovery of a wall of ice, 160 feet high and 500 miles long,
stunned and amazed readers just as revelations about the
Moon or Mars would thrill later generations. (The ice shelf,
the sea he navigated, and a prominent island were named
Ross in his honor.)

When Ross's fellow officer and Antarctic shipmate John
Franklin later headed to the Arctic in search of the Northwest Passage with *Erebus* and *Terror* and failed to return, Ross
bravely set out to find his friend. Ross and others did not suc-
ceed; evidence, facts of their last weeks, later offered a story of how Franklin and his men, after losing their ships to
the ice, set out on foot and perished. Death lurked, ever-at-
hand, along with polar explorers.

(Some years later, in 1905, a beak-nosed Norwegian named
Roald Amundsen climbed aboard an old fishing boat and
became first to bash through the Northwest Passage. Two
years of this three-year endeavor were spent on an Arctic island
where he and his small crew traded with the Inuit, absorbed

key polar survival skills from the locals, including the advantages of native cold-weather clothing. Amundsen would deploy this training when he set out for the South Pole.)

While the ship pitched and rolled southward, fifty degrees south, sixty degrees south, heading to the high seventies of southern latitude, my body adjusted to life at sea. One day, I taped an illustrated timeline of early twentieth-century Antarctic expeditions to the wall by my bunk. I like timelines not because of what they illustrate but for all the things they leave out, as though events exist outside of this world, untethered to a particular landscape, unmarred by human suffering or desire, as though events are unrelated, as though there is no knock-on effect or ripple effect or consequence. The notion of time as a line never resonated for me. Time for me appeared as a disk, an old 78 record album, slightly tilted, like the Milky Way.

In 1897 the Royal Geographical Society announced its intention to locate and claim the South Pole for Great Britain. Between 1901 and 1921, in twelve expeditions, men from Scotland, Japan, France, Australia, Norway, Germany, and Great Britain walked the ice in this pursuit. These stories form the spine of early twentieth-century Antarctic histories, peppered with bold innovations—polar explorers adapted new technologies under perilous conditions, which makes for interesting stories. For example, transport: Motorized vehicles were brought to Antarctica by Shackleton on the Nimrod expedition, even though they had yet to be fully integrated into more temperate societies. These were not men who believed in elaborate "practice runs" before the actual event. Many came to Antarctica having never skied before. Some see this as foolhardy. Others, such as myself, feel the wonder of their confidence.

The timeline centered on the "race" for the South Pole, which began in earnest in November 1901, when Scott, a midlevel English naval officer, sailed south with a purpose-built ship called Discovery.

Picture this: Between 1901 and 1912, four pole quests dominate the stories, two by Scott (accompanied on the first by his soon-to-be archrival Ernest Shackleton), one by Shackleton (where he came within ninety-seven nautical miles of the pole), and then—surprise!—Amundsen arrived, snatching the world's last great geographical "unknown" with formidable efficiency.

What struck was the high drama of it all—following the characters on an icy stage to their sometimes-tragic ends. Scott, an ambitious, doomed naval officer, whose big mistake may have been his refusal to use dogs to pull their South Polar–bound sledges. Instead, five men manhauled, yoking themselves to sledges weighing hundreds of pounds. They slowly perished on the return journey—one fell and hit his head, one wandered off because his frostbitten feet did not allow him to keep up, three were found in the tent the next spring, a mere eleven miles from a fuel and food supply depot that might have saved their lives.

In a short time, I came to know their stories as though I had heard them all my life.

Shackleton, an Anglo-Irishman by birth, is portrayed as offering inexhaustible good humor and devotion to his men. Shackleton never directly lost a man in his explorations. He died in 1922 when his heart gave out aboard a ship called the Quest, attempting one more Antarctic voyage.

Amundsen's Norwegian egalitarianism showed in how he offered his men equal part in the expedition—down to all holding the bamboo flagpole while ramming it into the ice, marking the South Pole for the first time. Amundsen vanished in 1928 while on an air reconnaissance mission looking for the Italian explorer Umberto Nobile, whose airship had crashed in the Arctic.

Both Scott and Shackleton had departed for the South Pole from Ross Island, where they built wooden huts. The huts remain largely intact a hundred years after their abandonment.

The timeline showed photos of the men, windburned, by these structures. I studied the photos, wooden, prefabricated buildings originally designed for Australian Outback settlers. The images defined raw fragility: the sharp contrast of silvered wood against all that ice. Why hadn't the ice flattened them, I wondered, or why hadn't they rotted?

But rot is an organic process, where bacteria or fungi slowly break things down. The Antarctic presented cold, dry air inhospitable to rot.

After a week, after our ship crossed the Antarctic Circle, we pushed into the Ross Sea. Empty yet full, white yet blue, ice-shrouded rock spreading out as far as the eye could see: I wrote about people living in capsule-like bases, what they ate and read and how they planned booze rations using accountants' spreadsheets and grew pot in their hydroponic greenhouses for sustenance through the sensory-depriving winter darkness.

The landscape overwhelmed. I spent my first Antarctic week walking between the Greenpeace base and the historic Scott hut, side by side at Cape Evans. Scott's hut—a word used to signify temporary or makeshift shelter and not one offering the right resonance for a place where men survived all that cold and ice—was an insulated wooden dwelling, a prefabricated place with a frontier aesthetic. The Greenpeace base followed a mobile-classroom aesthetic, painted a sickly shade of yellowish green, a color announcing that the paint was donated not selected. I don't know what I expected, but it all seemed so flimsy and crude, it approached the feeling of a stage set.

The electric-orange Greenpeace helicopter roared back and

forth to the ship, delivering food and generators and canned peaches. You could see the rosy fruits' bright labels levitating off the deck, in nets slung under the helicopters. The two pilots, Gary and Roger, were brave men who spent most of their free time tending the helicopters' engines and rotor blades. Aviation was behind many of the Antarctic's most perilous and lethal human stories, crashes caused by extreme cold, poor visibility, and pilot error, distances being mirage-like across the homogenous white, compasses made irrelevant by the close proximity of the magnetic South Pole.

The Ross Sea in summer, bathed in twenty-four-hour sunlight, made a brilliant liar out of anyone who called the place gray, lifeless, bitter cold. The sunlight inspired people, fueled bounteous energy. Loading and unloading, zipping across choppy seas in gray inflatable boats, measuring effluent in beakers and test tubes, stacking canned tomatoes into an ice cellar. We walked around in T-shirts and snow pants, then relaxed on the peeling paint of the sun-warmed metal deck, at anchor, sipping rum splashed over ancient ice. We drank Antarctica.

"We could make a lot of money," said Toby, a blond, Swedish ship's engineer, during a session with Bundeberg Australian rum. Someone had found a lime and we tried to fashion mai tais. "Hauling this ice back to New York and London and selling it, 100 percent pure, unadulterated water, straight from millions of years of pristine cold storage."

Maggie, laughing, replied, "Listen mate, I don't think we're supposed to imagine how we can make money on all of this. We're supposed to be *saving* the world."

One morning the lead pilot, Gary—who worked as a heli-wrangler on Australian sheep stations—and I whirred aloft headed to the American megabase called McMurdo, or Mac-town. The volcano's steam a gossamer pennant. We wore Telex headsets, chatted about the sights—black rock against white ice, a new syntax of place, this immense, seamless display of the idea, *frozen solid.*

Gary talked to some American pilots on the radio. Don't land at McMurdo, was the message. Gary told them he could land wherever he wanted to, as dictated by the Antarctic Treaty. When we floated to the ground at Mactown, two Navy men and the base leader, a red-faced man named Ron, told us to go away. One of them said, "Get out of here!" like he was talking to a dog. I was ready to do as told; then Gary began reciting the Antarctic Treaty—standing tall, shoulders back in his orange survival suit, green aviator sunglasses glinting in the light, calm: We were entitled to land our helicopter there. It wasn't their land. "The Antarctic belongs to all of us." The men stepped aside, Ron muttered, "You better not bother anyone or go in our buildings! You won't find any diamonds or gold here!"

Mactown was a jumbled heap, office park meets college dorms meets mining camp: Muddy tracks between two-story prefabricated buildings and some Jamesways—the half-cylinder, corrugated metal gray buildings I associate with early airfields—it was a work in progress, added onto as needed, not following any overall plan or design. It was also the largest base in Antarctica. People came to McMurdo to go elsewhere—it was the main transit point for thousands of scientists heading into the field. All this had gone on for decades until one day Greenpeace and other environmental groups decided to show the world photographs: pipes pumping untreated sewage water into pristine McMurdo Sound and an open-pit dump gently spewing clouds of smoke over the hills.

Greenpeace had warned me that, as an American citizen on a U.S. facility, the McMurdo brass might try to push the law and formally charge me with trespassing. The New Zealand contractor who hired many of the cooks and truck drivers and mountain guides employed at McMurdo had sent out a blanket warning that anyone caught talking to us would be put on the first plane home. The United States Navy apparently issued a similar warning to their people. Some reporters like that sort of challenge. Not this one. I tried not to picture life at Leavenworth. I wrote stories about people and food and how ecosystems functioned. I had no interest in asserting my right to test the Antarctic Treaty system. I was a coward.

Yet once I walked away from the angry American welcoming committee, I felt strangely immune to their authority. I believe it was the sheer scale of the ice I observed, flying over from Cape Evans, offering a big wild statement about how I needed to transcend my small, cowardly tendencies. Think big, it urged. I trudged immediately to the dump and took some photos. A man with a long-lens camera stood on the dump's rim, above me—in size it reminded me of an excavation for a large office building—aiming his camera my way. I waved to him but felt strange, being observed and recorded. Who would be the audience for those photos?

Roy, a New Zealand geoscientist, had made it known that Greenpeace folks were welcome in his lab; when I knocked on his door, he offered me a cup of tea. Roy came south for several months a year, had done for three years, piecing together a geomorphological model of how New Zealand and Antarctica were once linked, all speaking to ideas of Gondwanaland, the southern supercontinent.

Roy poured milk into our steaming mugs, offered me chocolate cookies, and all the while explained how oil companies could use his work as they explored the region. I asked if they were indeed looking around for minerals to exploit and he laughed. "Of course they are! That's what they do, explore!"

His analysis showed matches between often-distant continents, offering proof of how these rocky terrains were once linked. If there is oil or natural gas in one place, its geochemical twin might offer the same. But work as a petrochemical assayer was not Roy's intent, regardless of what some environmentalists suggested.

His wife of a dozen years had left after he missed a third Christmas at home while working in Antarctica. "South polar explorers make bad partners," he said, half shrugging and looking out the window. "I love coming here. I cannot imagine not coming here."

"McMurdo's trash dump publicity," Roy added, "had people racing to get it tidied, hence the chilly response to Greenpeace—the group's surprise attack method left the Antarctic base managers feeling jumped and manipulated."

"All very embarrassing: We are trying to get it all cleaned up, but it's expensive and tedious—this stuff has been accumulating for decades. Stuff from the 1950s. Attitudes about trash and the environment and Earth Day—it took longer to reach us here at McMurdo. No malicious intent. We just kept operating under a 1962 ethic. Remember, too, nothing down here decays. To be scientists accused of ruining the very place you need millions of dollars to study, well . . ." his voice trailed off.

Roy sighed, leaned back in his chair. Like most men in Antarctica, he sported a big beard and a confusion of hair. Antarctica offers a fundamentally lonely face to people, he said, as I finished my tea.

I had a set rendezvous time with Gary and did not want to be late. Roy shook my hand and stood in the door of his Jamesway, waved, then disappeared inside. My boots splashed into black puddles reflecting a cloudless sky.

We lifted off from the icy helipad but our radios had ceased to function for reasons Gary couldn't determine. The ship had no idea where we were. Alone.

From the air, you read Antarctic's bigger story. Who cares about dumps and bilge water? Rock, splitting and drifting, still heaving its way out of an ice flood, rock sublimated by ice, the sea saturated with ice, sunlight pounding down all around, an unimaginable scale. Antarctic ice accumulated over millions of years, some to a thickness of two or three miles. Ninety percent of our ice and 70 percent of our fresh water were right there beneath me. *Antarctica.*

Our small crew documented immediate environmental pollution, like outflow pipes, but sailed to the Antarctic because of what Roy spoke of, the new Antarctic explorers, who wanted to extract minerals from the continent and its surrounding seas.

"Hey wait a minute!" Peter, the outraged Greenpeace Antarctic campaign leader would yelp during crew meetings. "They cannot have it because it is not *theirs.* It belongs to all of us. We say World Park International Preserve. Not bloody open-cast mines." Peter, a former London truck driver, was in Antarctica driven by a sense of moral outrage. He didn't like journalists, although he was quick to tell me it was, "nothing personal. You're just all owned by the companies you work for; look at all the business news you cover. Why not write that some of us don't want to live in a businessman's world? It's left to us to tell the world what is really going on down here, reporters won't come looking for this story."

While I found his subversive, anti-them diatribes strangely appealing, it would be dishonest not to admit that many days I wanted nothing to do with saving the world. I wandered around on the beach at Cape Evans. Ahead of me, the cold, blue waters of the Ross Sea, and to my right the newish Greenpeace hut with its wires, barrels, and latrines. To the left, the silvered wooden hut built by the men of *Terra Nova* as a way-station en route to the South Pole, a good place to contemplate life.

The only immediate threat beyond weather were the skuas, menacing birds that dive-bombed my head hoping for some tasty morsel, or circled penguin colonies, picking off chicks and eating them alive. I knew if I fell dead there, skuas would be happy to eat me too. Nature, hungry and indifferent, contrasted our ambition or desire to walk to the poles, to dig into the Earth's surface to recover shiny ores, coal, and oil and gas, pursuits of different generations, both shrouded in denial. At Cape Evans I wrote in my journal, *We dig and pull and pump out what we want, as though we desire the Earth to be a husk covered with a grid of roads, tracks, and runways.*

The Barne glacier's lines imprinted onto my retinas. The Barne a chunky, white cliff, supporting the White Cliffs of Dover analogy.

Antarctica's sound: Old air, trapped, ice melting and then the wheeze and pop of its escape. Water pushing ice. Distant skuas, penguins, talking among themselves. A generator cranking along. The whirring engines of boats going back and forth, ship to shore. The sound picture was not pure wilderness. Yet the human sounds gained no purchase on the cold, hard surface. People believe Antarctica is a difficult landscape to survive; yet the number 1 cause of death is industrial accidents at research bases, not falls down crevasses. Standing on the black beach, drinking coffee in a long undershirt and army fatigue pants, no hat, no gloves, knowing that soon the wind would come screaming down from the polar plateau. The wind and ice allowed me to stand on that beach, a great gift of stillness and sunshine in a place ready to define inhospitable.

Mount Erebus emerged as a fine companion for these meditations, ruling its planetary empire, a fire-filled crater in defiance to the ice terrain. Because of the environment's relative homogeneity—ice, sea, rock—a mild sense of boredom plagues most observers after the initial dazzle wears off. In our temperate world, small details animate each walk out of doors, leaves let go and move with the wind, squirrels hop erratically, a lonely river rises with the night's rain.

I remember the moment I stepped from this world fully into that world, when the Antarctic had me.

I could see a world erupt and glitter: The ruins of explorers' huts, the certainty of an ice blanket millions of years in existence, and penguins inverting the world—sea became sky. I held a palm-sized piece of ice, plate-glass clear, decorated with pinhole sized air bubbles, air transported to this time, Holocene, from another, Miocene, Pliocene, Pleistocene, put it in my mouth, and it tasted like the color blue. I became a polar explorer.

When we came home to Lyttelton, I did not get the chance to hear more of Baden's stories, or to even say good-bye. A crowd jammed the quayside, including people there to meet me. After six weeks at sea, and with another two and a half months looming after our resupply, I dove sobbing into a friend's arms on the dock, delighted and animated with stories of giant ice. All I could do was grab my pack and head off to the Southern Alps to hike. I missed the smell of wet earth.

Two weeks later we departed Lyttelton for a steam across the world's most remote seas, arriving in Ushuaia, Patagonia, before turning southward, to the South Shetland Islands and the Antarctic continent, where we stayed until the very edge of the austral autumn. During those months as we were at sea in the Southern Ocean, or running along the Antarctic coast, through architectonic ice, blue caverns, white arms, pocked and lavender in the sun, I stood on the deck in the cold, wet, winds and recalled Baden's stories of sailors who came south and the perfect instinct he had about their meaning—in historic accounts crewmen are portrayed as men without wills of their own, in no small part due to the fact that explorers often ran their crews like military operations.

Yet the seamen time and again met the physical and mental challenges of polar travel, creating with their bodies and minds the fabric of these polar narratives, stories that over time gave them at best a subordinate role and at worst erased them completely. This was something I had not fully grasped before—and grasped was the right word, because living in the Antarctic, while clearly possible and increasingly easy, would always require physical tenacity and a keen focus.

What Baden tried to depict in Lyttelton—in the photos of those long-dead sailors—was a subversive history of exploration—one that burst with extraordinary examples of selfless bravery, the ability of a man to bring on his best in situations of hair-raising peril, replete with hunger, madness, blackened frozen feet and the possibility of a slow, painful death.

What a contrast to the cleaner story of Antarctic exploration currently on offer—that of a "Heroic Age" of discovery evolving into a benevolent Antarctic world of international scientific cooperation. One where we see Antarctica as a place of wonder, a place seemingly created as backdrop or stage set, a place to challenge human character and intellect, a place where the Earth's great mysteries await our scrutiny. All we need to do is peel back the ice.

While steaming along the Gerlache Strait, we encountered three humpback whales, the great showmen of the cetacean world; breaching, flippers waving, they scooted alongside our ship in what felt strangely like a warm welcome. Maggie stood on deck and periodically nudged me, saying, *listen to them breathe.* Indeed, breath became the most captivating part of the engagement, exhaling great, oily blasts, smelling of fish and something foreign I could not identify. The whales were our sole conversation for a week as we called in at the British Antarctic Survey base named for Michael Faraday, a chemist and physicist (although in the nineteenth century, when he lived, his occupation was termed "natural philosopher"), to check their effluent. I found a cardboard scrap on the ship and wrote with a turquoise felt-tip pen: *Loneliness. Fantasy. Desire.* The Antarctic landscape came to inhabit me and I carried that sign in the map pocket of my blue Gore-Tex jacket as I traveled all over the world, and it was those words, more than any photo or cold-weather gear or conversation, that brought the Antarctic and all its mysteries back to the front of my mind.

At night I dream of Antarctica: Snow falls from a light sky, suspended, I drift. Far below, glaciers push out toward the sea. Muscles across my back contract and my arms are wings. I fly.

I am writing this in Christchurch, where I have just attended a conference on bioprospecting in Antarctica. Some loud debate at the dinner after the conference: Should companies be allowed to vector into Antarctica via various research programs to do research that may yield saleable compounds? It's already happening, one scientist said. Now it cannot be stopped. The argument for this work built around the idea that the private sector may be able to work in an accelerated way, to find that the cure for cancer exists in some benthic sea spider's enzymes. Government-sponsored research doesn't have this edge, someone else added, no clue how to make something practical out of the work on the ice. Government research has been too focused on "blue sky" speculations. Practical, one biologist said. What ever happened to the wonder of discovery? Why does it all have to be immediately applied to be valuable? Afterwards, I asked Alan Hemming about this discussion and he said that the only practical finding that he knew of, in spite of all the talk of a cure for cancer, is that pigments that make krill orange work well in lipstick and other cosmetics.

I dream. Sky pale, a mantilla of ice blossoms, web and shawl, spinning from some ghost-loom.

I am the ice and the ice is me.

Two

This is the period between life and death. This is the way the world will look to the last man when it dies.

　　　　　　　　　　　　　　　—Richard Byrd, *Alone* (1938)

Antarctic Peninsula; Fourth Month at Sea

On a cold April morning, I was about to set myself free, bound
for the Antarctic shore in a small inflatable boat, leaving
behind our rotund black, white, and ocher research ship
where I had lived for the past three and a half months, sway-
ing in the waves, in front of cliffs appearing hewn from slub
steel. We were at anchor, stopped, south of Argentina, south
of Drake's Passage, en route to a small research station further south still, to take a look at how people live on the Antarctic Peninsula. But we were in no particular hurry; it was
clear and reasonably warm for the early austral autumn, about
40 degrees Fahrenheit. We wanted to walk on land.

There were four of us headed to the island: Maggie, who
drove the inflatable; two scientists, Ingrid and Pablo; and Werner, who worked in the engine room and doubled as a "survival expert" for shore parties. Werner, an Austrian who pronounced his name with a V sound (Verner), began the same

lecture I heard on each of these shore-bound cruises. He was thin, maybe six feet tall, with deeply wrinkled skin, a gray afterthought of beard. He wore a bright orange survival suit, one that would float and keep the wearer alive for a few minutes if one were to hit the liquid-ice water. Mags wore one as well. Me, the reporter, and the two environmental scientists wore only our Gore-Tex parkas, fleece jackets, standard camping-store attire. No one spoke about how the life-extending gear was divvied up, why there wasn't more for everyone. It's just how it is.

Werner was OK until something went wrong. Then, as I witnessed over the months, hang on to your hat. Werner screamed, he waved his arms around wildly, he became a sort of Teutonic character speaking a mixed language, Germanglish. I first saw this side two weeks into the expedition, when he taught me how to steer the ship. Why a guy from the engine room was given the honor only occurred to me later. I had wanted to learn to steer. It looked fun and interesting and reminded me of all my favorite ahoy-matey tales, the stuff that satisfied my wanderlust when I was too young to act on it. I wanted to know what it felt like to steer the ship across the open ocean, to move past tabular icebergs alone in the sea. Who knew when I would get such an opportunity again?

Of course, no one needed to know that during the months at sea, I stretched out in my bunk each morning and discussed with God sinking ships, floating hopelessly alone on the sea, a watery death. God and I had cut a deal: Our ship would not sink, but if it did, I would be one of the people rescued. Sure, I told God, it would be harrowing if this had to happen, but when they shot off the pressurized containers, releasing the soft, lozenge-sided lifeboats, I would climb the ladder down the side of the ship, get in one, and then a helicopter would come and fish us out. I kept this mantra to myself, of course, because the idea that the helmsman was considering her abandon-ship routine at any moment while also trying to ease the vessel through floating ice or across dark and wind-blown seas might have been grounds to lose the privilege.

Work at sea was divided into four-hour shifts; working on the bridge was called "watch," and meant steering a one hour-long shift, shifting to the bridge deck and scanning the sea with glasses, coming inside and doing a fire watch below decks, closing doors knocked open by pounding seas, making tea and Milo, an Ovaltine-like malt drink, for the entire watch complement—in our case, four. I would begin my four-hour shift by conversing with God, not being in the moment, moving in the wheelhouse almost as if in a dream. I would look around and think, *Wow! This is great! Well, how did I get here?* Then focus on our rolling, how each one of us, four or six on the bridge, moving the same way to the same swells, moving across the water, hearing the mates, Bernadette or Ken or Bob, call out in British-accented curling words, from the chart room, "Steer 1–8–0, please." There was nowhere else for my mind to turn. Be here now. Now is the time.

When it was time, I pulled open the heavy door that lead to the outdoor bridge deck, slamming it shut, cut off from the wheelhouse. There had been no threat of being washed overboard, but I was careful to make a detailed assessment of wave motion. Was the main deck awash? How spiked did the waves appear? What else was out there with us, how much ice, how many yards, miles of tabular icebergs, calved from an ice tongue further south still, now roaming the frigid water, islands unto themselves. I am alive, I shouted into the cold wind that blasted my white cheeks while I stood on an anchor chain, looking through green field binoculars for ice in a sea of dark water, white foam and yes! Ice! I see it! I waved to the watch on the bridge, gestured the direction, ice coming, four points off the starboard bow, each piece a bit bigger than a rabbit. A herd of ice rabbits dancing across the water, dancing right along with me.

When I was to learn to steer, some time after I learned how to look for ice (look for the white that doesn't disappear, raising a new set of questions regarding absolute present tense. Disappear: to pass from view, to cease to be). The ship sported an old-timey wheel. The wheelhouse was forward on the ship, about a third of the length of the ship from the prow. The wheel was varnished, grainy hardwood, perhaps four feet across. People have held it like this for almost thirty years. It was not unlike driving an old standard-shift car, one where muscle matters. The wheel made itself known in a gentle, insistent tension, a weight, across the palms of my hands, I realized it was not the ship communicating with me on these hands, but the sea. I held the wooden wheel, which had singular, carved handles. It was harder to turn than I expected, a sort of pushing back, the kind of tension you get when you lean into someone unexpectedly on a rocking train. "Pardon me," the ship seemed to say, "you're stepping on my foot." I watched the compass spin, encased in glass, like a snow globe for a child, only this one spun and when it settled it told you where you were headed, because in the biggest, darkest, roughest sink on the planet, there were no road signs, and the celestial road map was lost under steely clouds, so we were left with our faith that Ken and Bernadette and Bob really did know how to do the math that allowed a ship to travel in a straight line using a compass, which appears in the Bible, in II Kings, meaning a curved or roundabout course, but for us meaning destiny, hope, the 32 points of a 360-degree circle. I watched it spin, far from the heading called out to me by the mate, Bob, who offered to let me learn to steer on his watch.

"So Werner," I said, "how do you know how much to turn the wheel if you are aiming for a five-degree course correction?"

Werner began to tell me about this, but the mate interrupted. It was Robert Graham's watch, Black Bob as he was known, and the night before he was rumored to have grabbed the cook and told her to stop making so much rice. "Me and the mates want potatoes," he said. Vicky, the cook, who came to us via Girl Scout camps in the western United States, and cooked like someone whose menu was limited to a twelve-year-old's palette, had made rice for three consecutive nights.

Bob was in the chart room, adjacent to the bridge, and he called out our course: 1–7–8. I turned the wheel, watching the snow globe ease toward 1–7–8 and thinking about what a natural I am as an able-bodied seaman. Maybe I was a sailor in a past life, I mused. Maybe . . . But my thoughts were interrupted. The compass continued to climb. How odd, I thought. I wondered how turning the wheel such a small amount could cause this . . . a rough, firm voice called out, "Where are we?"

I called back, "1–8–5, sir." But the compass continued to swing, each ascendance my doom. 1–9–0, 1–9–5. This ship, this fat tug, was suddenly threading the needle in the cresting waves of the Southern Ocean and we took the waves abeam, or at a perpendicular angle. This was bad. As the ship started to slam and things begin falling off shelves, people became nauseated, and worst of all there was a distinct, endless smacking sound, reminding us all where we were and what was out there, on the other side of the ship's metal shell. Bob stood, unfazed, behind me.

"What in the bloody hell are you doing?" His voice contained little emotion; he almost seemed to be smiling. It was, you could say, merely a simple question inviting an equally simple answer.

The compass reels along 1–9–5 long gone, into the 2–0–0s. The numbers climbed. The ship pounded by the seas.

"I can't steer," I half shrieked. "I think someone else better take the wheel."

When I let go with my right hand, Bob put it back into place and impassively stated, "You will stay on the wheel until relieved."

While I heard this, I didn't quite understand. Clearly, I was not a sailor in a past life. Was that not clear to all aboard? Clearly, I was not good for our general well being.

The clock told me there were forty-five more minutes ahead. I stayed put.

Werner stood to my right, talking fast. "Ease her back to the starboard. I mean move her to your port. Or your left. Whatever seems easier for you to remember. Too far! Ease it back the other way! Too far! You're overcorrecting! We'll be feeling the waves again from the other side."

Minutes crept by; we were still not on course. We were pounded by the sea. Boom! The stairway door opened and the first mate, Ken from Didcot, England, appeared. There remained tension between the colonials (being the Kiwi Bob, the Americans, the Australians) and the English on the ship. He shook a big head of gray curls.

"Oh," he said, looking at me and smiling, "it's you. I was wondering who was making the ship do a 180. I thought Bob was enjoying too many sneaky coffees."

He smiled at his own sly humor, and gently ran his tongue over the gummed edge of a cigarette paper, then lit a spindly homemade cigarette.

"Skipper wants me to stay up here for a while."

I glanced at Bob, whose face looked redder than usual. What an insult! Mates never oversaw each other's work. I felt the sweat on my palms, and Bob stared straight ahead. "Steady there," he said in my general direction. I wiped my palms, one at a time, on my Gore-Tex jacket, wondering why in the world no one seemed inclined to step in, Werner excluded. Jumped. Waved his arms. Ken's face was frozen in his trademark taciturn smile. The others on the watch, two Spaniards and another American, stared out the bridge windows, smoked, gazed at the horizon. Time stopped. I was alive.

No one mentioned the bad steering ever again. My name appeared on the next day's chore and duty roster, a roster made by Ken. I was on as a wheelman with the "twelve to four," Bernadette's midnight to four a.m. and the noon to four p.m. watch.

As we zoomed toward shore, Werner began the list. "Do not wander off. Do not interfere with the environment. Do not take anything or leave anything behind. If you must smoke," he added, looking at me with narrowed eyes, "you must take all the paper and tobacco back to the ship." I smiled at him, my winsome American smile that said, yes, I do know this rule, after three months of it. But I knew Werner was not mean, he was Austrian and could not help himself. Rules matter.

Maggie nosed the boat in toward the rocky edge that served as landing spot. We had a joke, she and I. No matter how many survival expert–hippie–environmental scientists were in the boat, they all sat there trying not to be the first one out. They didn't want to get wet. So they waited to see if someone else would get out first, grab the painter and pull, heave ho!, the small craft to shore. Maggie and I no longer cared for the suspense. When we headed ashore, I always rode in her boat, sat in front, and rested my knees against the inflated section forming the prow. She stood at the stern, eyes to the shore, no-nonsense and all concentration. Those boats don't flip easily, but you come in on a bad beach where there's a sharp drop off and suddenly people were hopping out into ten feet of frigid water.

As we edged toward the rocky shore, I looked back and she nodded, looking very Steve McQueen. At her signal, I hauled my backpack on and perched myself, poised to push off and away from the boat, snag the painter and then heave-ho while she yanked up the prop and waded up to help. The scientists, who included a chubby Argentine and a lame-legged Belgian, pulled bits and pieces of things out of Ziploc plastic bags. When we secured the boat, Maggie radioed in to the ship. They could see us from the bridge on what was a perfectly bright and still and wildly monochromatic day, except for the water, which defiantly refused to go to black. It said, hey, I am azure, I am cobalt. Come on over and stare down to the bottom. I am air. See through me.

Werner told us routinely not to go out alone, to always take a survival pack and a buddy. But after months of warnings and knowing that people were no more than one-hundred yards behind the next hill, I needed to break out.

"This is the Antarctic," the Survival Guys liked to murmur. There were three of them on the ship, two were serious mountain climbers when not doing Greenpeace work. Serious being the fact that this is what they listed as their occupation, when I passed around a sheet asking people what their shore jobs happen to be. Mountaineer. Serious also being a $40,000 debt they owed on a climb that went bad. How bad? I had asked. One of the guys in their party lied about his experience. They were in the Himalayas, high above the clouds. They could see from his panic he had no idea what to do at that altitude. There was nothing to do but come down.

Check your packs. And recheck your packs and never let the shore or the ship out of your sight. In the Antarctic, if you forget something or you get lost, you die.

When the boat was secure, I lit a cigarette with Mags in the protective shadow of a rock. The worst thing that had happened so far was running out of beer and potatoes for a while. Then it was port o' call Ushuaia, Patagonia. But those last few days had counted as distress on board, after almost three weeks steaming from New Zealand, no land and finally, no beer in sight. Emergency drills implemented, squads of bushy-haired forty-and fifty-year-old men, wearing tie-dyed T-shirts stating "Water for Life" ripped into supply closets, swearing and shouting that there must be some overlooked cases of Double Brown and Steinlager. Real emergencies of the gut.

Mags headed off to look at an iceberg grounded, rotting, a hundred yards up the coast. I turned and walked in the opposite direction. Werner was perched on a nearby ice hill, surveying the still water. Most likely looking for whales, I reckoned.

I walked for ten, twenty, thirty minutes. I wore old Timberland boots, in a light yellow-beige suede, boots I had bought at L.L. Bean in Freeport, Maine, on a weekend trip with my uncle Peter, boots that had seen wide stretches of the Appalachian Trail in Virginia, and in Maine they hiked the snowy, boulder-strewn flanks of Mount Katahdin, trudged along the steep, bush-covered trek over Arthur's Pass in New Zealand, trod the red Nullarbor Plain of Australia, ambled in the Andean foothills. Those boots meant business. They kept my feet warm and dry and were also aesthetically pleasing to me. I disliked the rubber and fleece and super-fiber Vibram-soled space shoes worn by the crew. They looked like they were about to walk on Mars, dressed as some 1950s kid would imagine a spaceship crew to look. No, these boots are leather and worn and have covered ground on every continent in the world. They offer me the promise of experience and the hold of an old friend's hand.

I looked about but the rest of the shore party was nowhere in sight. We had a couple hours alone, then more boats would appear, with more people from the crew. My window for solo exploration was narrow, so I walked carefully but quickly over the rocky beach strewn with chunks of ice. I rounded the corner and stopped.

Before me they rose. Bones. An immense skeleton, stretching along the shore in front of me. The individual vertebrae the size of softballs, growing to the size of coffee tables. I stepped into the tail. Picked my way through vertebrae, touched enormous ribs stretching toward the sky. They were wearing in the cold, salty air, and their surface was gray, rough, pocked with caverns, holes where black grit has taken residence. It was big, crazy, a Georgia-O'Keefe-meets-Robert-Motherwell moment, curvilinear forms twisting over black rock, fist-sized chunks of ice and all pinned down by a nickel-plated sky.

I stepped back outside the enormous ribs. I touched one arch, felt deep dives, resonating with power, and wit, and gentle understanding, all the things I'd been told whales possess. While whales did not hold me in their thrall, I had discovered kinship with them while at sea. You might even say I sensed what it was like to live as they did, owning the ocean in their "hey, I'm as big as a football field" way. Part of me lingered, contemplating the rude end so many met, oil, bone, sushi.

I wondered how this particular whale met its fate, and how long it had taken for all not bone to dissolve away. Whales. Perfect for ocean, big, immensities that dive and move and sing across water that conducts sound farther than air.

But only bone remained. Things in Antarctica don't decay the way they do in more temperate climes; they sort of freeze dry and tighten. Dead animals end up looking like the mother stored in the fruit cellar in Psycho, the work of an amateur taxidermist who was not entirely sure how to make a lifelike rendition. But this skeleton was picked clean.

It was a cold day on the beach, colder than I thought and the ends of my fingers were getting the familiar sensation of sorry, blood is now being diverted to essential organs, brain, liver, heart. It was the wind really; the air was almost balmy when it stopped, but the wind wanted to blow in a non-pattern of strong gusts and still. The shore was not sandy, it was a narrow, steep incline of volcanic rocks and ground up rocks. It was hard to walk along, not strolling, more picking my way along the fringe, eyes focused on the chunks, which in the glowing pale of this overcast day look entirely unremarkable.

Across this narrow finger of sea were enormous cliffs that rose and were lost in a thick foglike cloud belt. When we arrived in the early dawn, it was a brilliantly sunny late afternoon, the light was purple and maroon and tangerine, and the clouds were so much tulle thrown down over this quilt of rock and light and texture.

Light does strange things at 65 degrees south. Whatever impressionist canvas I saw in the morning light was gone. In its place, a different story, a landscape reminding me that people do come here and get lost and freeze to death, looking up at those same black and white and indifferent cliffs.

I wanted to walk all the way to the point, to see how the land curled back on both sides, to see if any icebergs were floating on the horizon. As I got into rhythm on the sloping shore, I cast my eyes forward and saw, perhaps not twenty yards away, a long black seal, head resting on the ground.

Dead? It was curled in a most unnatural way, head extended forward onto the rocks, hindquarters hiked in the air. It must smell me, Gore-Tex and Velcro and Capilene and polar fleece and mint-flavored lip balm. It lifted its head in panic, throwing a narrow, pointed snout around, fixing black eyes on me, opening its mouth and making a sound so unlike anything I had ever heard, a moaning screaming fury. I stopped when I was within ten yards because the seal started to move. Once I watched a leopard seal, a carnivorous variety, chase and attack like a dog when one of my shipmates threatened to come too close. It was the strangest animal attack I had witnessed, how amazingly swift the seal moved across the ice, how wide its mouth opened, how firmly it bit this young

Swede's leg. Who would have thought that seals were fast on the attack when they were out of the water?

But this was a Weddell seal, or a crabeater, not the sort that has large, fang-like teeth and a desperate thirst for blood. I squatted down, watching her try to move. There was a deep indentation in her back; it looked like someone had taken a two-by-four and struck her solidly across the spine, leaving behind a deep furrow.

Most likely she was attacked by an orca or a large leopard seal and somehow managed to escape an immediate death. But it was clear she was on her way out, she knew it, I knew it, and she was there on a steep and unforgiving shore waiting to die, alone.

For reasons that remain unclear, this made me both angry and sad. I began to cry, wiping my nose on my blue Gore-Tex sleeve, listening to the poor miserable bitch's lonely baying. I wondered if I should kill her. Find a rock, pound her head in? What then?

I thought of the doctor on the ship. Maybe she could put the seal to sleep, injecting her with a dose of morphine and bring all this to a close. But I knew no one would go for that. We weren't supposed to take rocks, let alone wheel ourselves into assisted suicides for doomed marine mammals.

No, I was alone and powerless in this company. She rested her head on front flippers, eyes watching me and offering no sign of her thoughts,

So. I saw how the beach would change, adding something new, something old to its collection. And the newest piece would rest there, another hundred or more years as the salt air gradually ground bone to powder.

But first there would be the moment when time stopped for those eyes, when they no longer registered the color and smell of the world and then all the cells of that form would join the cascade of mortality. Oily skin collapsing into a hollow,

fleshy flippers evaporating into stiff side boards, all the promise of the ocean and the hunt and the rolling, tumbling ecstatic
engagement with sea and air washing away in the end.

I pulled out my Olympus OM-1, a camera that gets the job
done on days when fancy wholly electronic machines seize
up in the cold. I shot black-and-white with a variety of colored filters, which add a depth and richness and will, I hope,
give newspaper readers some sense of what this place is. I
knew the words already began to escape me. I screwed on a
28 millimeter lens, squatted on my haunches, took several
wide-angle shots of the seal in her final resting spot. Then I
changed to the 70 millimeter and came in close on her face.
She was tired, annoyed, enraged that I have added a further
dimension of menace to her deathbed.

I stopped shooting, finished making notes about the frames
and the time and place and the camera lens and film used. I
scratched out some words, I write: *I came upon a seal with a broken back. Maybe some other meaning? Weave into longer narrative
about the unforgiving nature of the Antarctic?* The seal watched
me from the corner of her eye, head resting on front flippers.
She looked like a big, fat, hairless dog. "There is nothing I
can do for you, my friend," I said aloud. As I picked my way
back toward the skeleton, I heard her expel a loud breath,
turned and saw a cloud of wet white vapor float from her
nostrils, head resting on flippers.

I returned to the whale, stood again in the rib cage. I cannot touch the sides or top when I am on the largest vertebrae. I am Jonah. I bent my head back, arching, bright-pink
gloved hands meeting, hanging on to one another. The bones
extended upwards with me, curling and enclosing me. Whales
sing different songs depending on where they live, songs
changing continuously and individual singers adopting new
material, singing in units, for hours, sometimes for days. I
balanced on a chunky piece of vertebrae, an ottoman of bone,

part of the triptych, me all the way in, the seal stepping out, whale long since vanished. I continued to stretch, hold my hands over my head and arch back until the horizon seems to reorient itself, the entire Earth and sky.

Field Notes

The ice changes by flowing out like a river toward the sea. Glaciers and ice tongues calve into the sea and then great landscapes of ice circulate on the ocean's currents.

There are 7 million cubic miles of ice in the Antarctic. No new water is created. The same water since the beginning. The ice of Antarctica changes the earth's shape, flattening the south polar end, giving our ball a slight pear shape.

Glacier. The people I sailed with said glah-see-er and mocked the American glay-shur. I still hear glah-see-er when I see the word on a page.

I thought about this one morning, or perhaps it was one sunny night, when a chunk of neighborhood ice, called Barne, cleaved off. It sounded like dynamite in a cartoon. A rumble and then pow! Cracking, waves, the Ross Sea rippling like a great carpet shaken out on a stone floor.

I sat alone watching this and I felt the narcotic effect of the wild. I considered how most of us come from towns pushing out into fields and woods, towns rebuilt over old ones, a plan called cover over, plough under, morph a string of fiberglass and vinyl and particle board across the landscape. How we destroy to acquire. How we flatten in one great acquisitive motion.

How water carves and changes rock because it moves and the rock may not, how the water has all the time in the world and keeps pressing on, picking up sand or falling from the sky onto an ice plateau at the bottom of the world. Water once understood to be locked into place at the bottom of the world.

Until the end of the twentieth century when Antarctica began to tell a different story entirely, as the ice began to collapse and break apart because something had begun to accelerate—something with a name and a story all its own. Cassandra-like, remote scientific bases in Antarctica began to narrate this new world, one of global climate instability. Decades would pass before a broad audience would parse the pieces and listen. That is, decades would pass before people other than those on a Greenpeace ship would listen. In 1988, when they told their story of an embattled Antarctic, their fight fell into the category of obscure environmental campaign. Two decades later, their quest appears more prophecy than performance.

Three

Crevasses are dangerous, especially when travelling in vehicles. . . . Snow bridges link crevasses; some bridges will take the weight of a vehicle, others will not take any weight at all. The essential rule is play safe. It is easier to avoid a crevasse than to get out of one!

—Field Manual, Antarctica New Zealand (1996)

Lyttelton, New Zealand

Fifteen years after Baden and I first met in the Lyttelton Museum, I phoned him from my Iowa home. My own Antarctic explorations had been moving slowly forward during those years, the lure of that landscape propelling me to quit my job as a magazine editor in San Francisco and begin work on an MFA—essays centered on how people place themselves amidst the ice and the stories that came of those explorations. My friends in San Francisco had been perplexed. My father, never one to soft-pedal, said bluntly, "I think this sounds like a big mistake."

Iowa, however, turned out to be a launchpad for my return to New Zealand—and Antarctica. Encouraged by the poets and essayists that populate that unusual Midwestern enclave of artists and writers, I wrote to Fulbright and asked for a grant to research little-known Antarctic histories in Christchurch. A year later they called from New York: Yes.

Baden recalled our first meeting. "Well," I said, "I guess I'll be around darkening your door for a year or so."

It was a clear, hot summer day in Christchurch when I arrived at the Canterbury Museum, a Gothic revival building designed by Benjamin Woolfield Mountfort in 1867, and framed by Hagley Park with its bright turquoise art-deco fountain. It is said Christchurch is more English than England, and as I walked toward the museum, across the Avon River then past the red telephone boxes long disappeared from London, I took it all in: the statue of Robert Falcon Scott along the Avon, a marble likeness carved posthumously by his wife, a sculptor who had once studied with Rodin. I stopped and admired him, looking out to some distant horizon, as a tram trundled past, tourists snapping his photo.

In his capacity as Canterbury's Antarctic curator and main Antarctic historian, Baden had guided tours and gathered artifacts and planned exhibits across several decades—and escorted heads of state and royal personages such as Prince Philip and Princess Margaret and an endless line of famed explorers' relatives from Scott's son Peter to Shackleton's granddaughter Alexandra—to portray how the Antarctic was imagined and explored. When he began doing this in the 1960s, he had few Antarctic museum colleagues in the world.

On weekends, Baden drove over the hills to the tiny Lyttelton Museum, where he portrayed another view of the same times—this time with an emphasis on the simple seamen who worked the ships and came to call Lyttelton home.

Time had not changed Baden—he remained fit, tan, and silver-haired.

"Who did you sell your soul to?" I asked as we shook hands.

"I was going to ask you the same question," he said, winking.

Baden had recently stepped down as Antarctic curator, although he assured me this seemed to mean little in terms of work.

"I do all the same things as before except now they don't pay me," he said with a smile. When he retired, they feted him at Warner's, the same restaurant on Christchurch's main square that Scott had used for his own farewell banquet, a room visited as pilgrimage by polar workers and scientists as they headed south.

Baden invited me to join a Polar Gallery tour about to begin. When the Polar Gallery first opened in the 1970s, His Royal Highness, the Duke of Edinburgh, came to town for the event. As we climbed the stairs, Baden told me about the renovation plan afoot to extend the museum. If this happened, the Polar Gallery would be redone. More of their best-in-the-world collection of Heroic Age gear would be out in the light and air. They planned to modernize how the stories were told. Good-bye to walls of glass cases filled with stuffed penguins, dogs, and small, handwritten cards describing it all, welcome new media displays, video, sound, recorded voices, facts, and quizzes.

"They want it to be more interactive, more geared towards children," Baden said. "I can't blame them, but I don't see why we can't challenge children today to animate ideas with their imaginations, rather than doing it for them with computers."

"At least you are open-minded," I said. He rolled his bright blue eyes. "Well, I am out of it now, let them do what they want." Before the tour began, Baden showed me two new pieces acquired at a recent auction—Scott's last train ticket, purchased in Australia as he traveled the countryside raising money for his explorations, as well as an unusual fragment of early polar life: a newsletter called The Blizzard. It had been carefully produced on a printing press brought to Antarctica by Ernest Shackleton, and Baden believed a mere fifty were printed; he knew only two other copies in the world, so it was an important score for Canterbury. *The Blizzard* represented one of the earliest moments of an ongoing Antarctic tradition, the creation of local news for polar inhabitants, Antarcticans reporting on their life and culture.

In the twenty-first century, the Internet-linked Antarcticans and their continent through Web sites called 70 South, antarctic-circle, and antarcticsun, not to mention scores of blogs and video blogs. All the major science programs offered Antarctic reports, including the British Antarctic Survey's web page, Penguin of the Day.

Forty tourists traveling with Elderhostel in sensible white track shoes and purple warm-up suits awaited Baden. He wore a microphone while the coach driver held a wireless speaker at the back of the crowd. Baden had a narrative line he followed, which he altered for the age of the crowd—children were more interested in penguins than people, Baden once said, adding with an agreeing nod, fair enough—and he tried not to run over the allotted time.

Most of the tour groups had busy days, he noted, first Canterbury, then off to the International Antarctic Centre at the airport, which was privately owned and run in conjunction with Antarctica New Zealand, the government department that managed New Zealand's Antarctic interests. The airport museum told the story of the Antarctic's environment and its role in all the Earth's systems, and explained how and why scientists explored the landscape. Human history had been represented in a Disney-like room where a reproduction polar hut surrounded by fake snow served as scene while an English voice of gravitas read from Robert Falcon Scott's journals, a mixture of creepy and corny, I had found. (Many of Scott's final entries seem almost too poetic for a man who was waiting to die. I have often wondered, although there is no evidence to support this thinking, whether he and his best friend the playwright J. M. Barrie hadn't dreamed up what one might write for posterity's sake, back when they would sit by the fire until all hours in London, sipping brandy. I wonder if Scott did not have a sort of mental script of how he would detail his end, how he would perform "hero" until his last breath. They planned their china, stationery, and every scrap they ate: Why wouldn't they have begun scripting their words, memoirs being a primary moneymaker for explorers? Of the three men who died in the tent, Scott was believed to have perished last. When they found their bodies, Scott had thrown back his sleeping bag, exposing himself to cold as though to say to Antarctica, *make haste now, there is but me; take me, I am yours.*)

Baden began with the story of Nicolai Hansen, the first person to study Adélie penguins in Antarctica. Hansen fell ill while doing so as part of the first party to ever winter-over south of the Antarctic Circle—the year was 1899. Hansen told his mates he would just like to hang on until the date the penguins returned from the sea. When they came up to Ridley Beach, an Adélie was brought to him and Hansen ran his hand down the back of its feathers. Hansen then died, securing his place as both the first to die in Antarctica while exploring and the first to be buried there.

Baden explained the museum's intimate ties with polar exploration; how these early explorers used the Canterbury Museum as a workplace. The museum was then closely linked to the University of Canterbury, across the street. The matching Gothic Revival buildings were converted into the Arts Centre in the 1970s when the university moved to the suburbs, and science labs became studios where fudge, kiwi-bird themed ceramic mugs, and sheepskin cell phone covers were made and sold.

Scott and his naturalist Edward Wilson worked in the

Canterbury Museum for six weeks in 1904, during the *Discovery* expedition, preparing penguin skins and writing reports on their findings. Sleds, skis, and dog harnesses from this expedition were then donated as a gesture of thanks for the New Zealanders support. The museum staff stored it all in the basement, and the relics of early explorations were largely forgotten until the 1970s.

Baden pointed out specific objects to the tour, including the dogs' medicine chest, reminding us of the dogs' tremendous role in opening Antarctica to humanity. "Very little of it would have been possible without them," he said.

The Polar Gallery deploys these objects with all their weird and quirky stories: the official portrait of Captain Scott, the first man awarded Great Britain's Polar Medal, and how the painter erroneously depicted the medal as round rather than as octagon. The quest for the South Pole was laid out as an intertwined biography of three men. Scott tried, Shackleton tried, but the Norwegian Amundsen came from nowhere and grabbed the crown.

"Of course, time had shown this Anglocentric polar history to be wildly skewed," Baden offered. Amundsen had hardly snuck in from nowhere, having already bashed through the Northwest Passage, and he did announce, albeit rather circumspectly, his intentions to reach the pole.

Baden detailed the gentlemanly order of early exploration. The British felt the South Pole was their cherry, and their dueling explorers, Shackleton and Scott, traded notes about where they proposed exploring, such as which specific routes they would follow. They would then agree who got to set up camp where. All very formal and polite.

"Yet these men despised each other," Baden added, but propriety demanded they stay in touch about the attack on the South Pole.

That afternoon in Canterbury, I gazed into the case

containing Amundsen's knife, a common seaman's tool, a pocket knife, a blackened version of a Swiss Army knife, and listened to Baden tell its story.

It had become common for Baden, during his four decades working in Antarcticana, to receive notes from people with possible polar relics—often penned by people who had stumbled across a mysterious piece in the attic, or among grandfather's papers hidden under a bed.

Baden offered how just such a note arrived from a Mrs. Rosen in America, "detailing a seaman's pocket knife, which she said had been used by Amundsen to cut the first flagpole erected at the South Pole."

Along with it came a letter from Amundsen himself, testifying that this was indeed true. Baden flew to San Francisco where he was directed in writing to leave a check at a certain hotel's desk. Having done so, a package containing the knife was delivered to him. He then carried it home to New Zealand in his pocket.

The knife was perhaps his favorite object in the entire collection. Amundsen carrying that knife back from the South Pole, where it had been messily scratched with the words Sud Polin and the date, represented something else entirely, the idea that a simple knife could animate the world's last, great terrestrial land-grab.

The knife, a blubber-blackened tool, ready to do its work, sat separated from the world behind a glass wall.

Behind it, Baden had pasted a black-and-white photo of the British team arriving a month after Amundsen. I have studied many heroic images of polar exploration, and I cannot say it is easy to register the emotions often consigned to them in captions, bitter disappointment, hope, reflection. Mostly, the people look cold and battered, and their skin transfixes with both its newly ebony hue and its shiny quality, like the Antarctic believes the men to be stones and polishes them with the wind.

Baden shed new light on this one: Scott and his four mates, all soon to be dead, standing and seated, all without beards.

"Why are they clean shaven at the South Pole? They should be sporting a great beard!" Baden challenged the group. "I'll tell you. Scott ran his ship by Royal Navy rules and these dictated men sign a contract about facial hair. You were either clean shaven or sported facial hair. Once you chose, you could not switch during the course of an expedition." Baden paused. "I have always wondered this: One reason these men died was because they ran out of fuel. They used vital fuel to shave. It is one of the great 'Ifs' of Antarctica—what if they had not shaved? Would they have lived?"

We then studied a small stove, called a primus, still the standard of backcountry campers and explorers. In addition to dogs, the primus made polar travel possible. "Perfected in Stockholm in 1896, it was no coincidence that the depth and breadth of polar fieldwork expands after this innovation," Baden added: "It was the key technology in South Polar exploration."

We all stared at the small device. The card next to it read, "This small pressure-stove travelled with Shackleton in the James Caird, 885 miles from Elephant Island to South Georgia, after the crushing of his ship, Endurance, in pack ice during the 1914–1916 Imperial Trans-Antarctic Expedition."

Nearby, a strange wooden wheel ringed by a rusting, medieval-looking metal tread—from the first motorized transport used in Antarctica. "Shackleton modified an Arrol Johnson motorcar before bringing it south during his 1907–1909 trip, for this he is considered the father of mechanization in Antarctica," Baden added.

In the center of the floor, on a raised platform, stood the motorized sledge Shackleton brought for the 1914–1916 trans-Antarctic crossing. The men marching across from the Ross Sea tried to use it with bad results.

I wandered away from the group, peering into cases containing tiny, delicate espresso cups, etched sherry glasses, white plates painted with expedition logos. For many years, the Antarctic story had been one of three, five men. The idea, presumably, is that these leaders stand in for the many who came along with them, furling the sails, stoking the fires, charting the courses, slinging the hash. Yet this left me unsatisfied. I wanted to know more about the men who were not the fundraisers, the icons of bravery and service to realm. I wanted to know about the men who came south and made nothing from the endeavor, who turned around and headed off to sea again when they returned home.

By the time I stepped back into Baden's group, they had reached the late 1950s. Baden was explaining how Vivian "Bunny" Fuchs, the English archaeologist and explorer, and Edmund Hillary, the New Zealand–born conqueror of Everest, set off to do what Shackleton first dreamed: An overland crossing of the continent. In the gallery, their two distinct vehicles; Able, an orange Sno-cat built in Oregon and originally designed to work on remote power lines in the western United States, and a red-and-yellow Massey Ferguson farm tractor, outfitted with clunky metal tread belts. This was how they reached the South Pole. The farm tractors driven by a game crew of New Zealanders with air support got there first, giving the British their second beating, and taking the honor of first motorized vehicle to the pole. Beside the tractor, the corporate sponsor BP's ads from the time: *Got man to the South Pole first!*

We ended the tour with Baden sharing stories of the historic huts built by Shackleton and Scott. When Baden worked at the huts in the early 1960s, they used dogs, fed them seal meat, and the task of procuring this meat revolted him. "This was horrible; the edge of the ice is total safety for seals. They recognize no danger. You'd shoot one and the one next to it would go back to sleep. It was quite an experience for me. They would have a permit to shoot thirty, to feed the dogs for the season, and they would try to do it all in one day." You could see the listeners shift uncomfortably from foot to foot. Baden noted this and added, "Our policy was shoot only aging males. Having reached that stage in my own life, I am not sure that's a very good idea."

We all laugh; seals shot dead fade, Baden makes penance for his killing—the seals are not forgotten, they join the weave of story—and we all head off to the café for a hot cup of milky tea.

Field Notes

The Norwegian shipmakers Wilhelmsen and Wilhelmsen had donated a fine bronze bust of Amundsen to the Canterbury Museum. Over the years so many people had touched his beakish and prominent nose that it glistened like a beacon. Why, I wondered, did people stroke his nose like that? Baden recounted how this began because of a story he concocted to fill time. A large group of Royal Thai Air Force airmen were in town and the museum's theater was too small to accommodate all of them for a single showing of the film on offer. So the airmen were divided into smaller groups, and some filed into the theater while some were left to wander the museum collections. Baden told them while they waited that anyone who rubbed Amundsen's nose received a special magic yielding a first-born son. Baden found this explanation funny and quickly told the airmen it was a joke—to this day, he told me, "I wonder what prompted me to say that." It was too late. Each year, dozens of Thai airmen trained in New Zealand, and they dutifully made a beeline to the shrine of Amundsen's nose.

Edgar Allen Poe wrote The Narrative of Arthur Gordon Pym in 1838, as the world pressed toward Antarctica's icy shores. Poe would have read whaler's stories of the icy Southern Ocean, and the stories of ships vanished rounding Cape Horn. While the Antarctic had existed in discussion and writings since the time of Aristotle, by the nineteenth century, stories began to reveal its strange details, the twenty-four-hour sunshine, the enormous waves, green icebergs the size of a Baltimore neighborhood. Pym, through a series of misfortunes in twenty-seven narrative sections, makes his way to Antarctica. Pym finds himself on the edge of the South Polar abyss. It's a spooky, white world, reminiscent of Dante's ice center of the Inferno, Melville's white whale, and from more modern times the white space station seen in Tarkovsky's film version of Stanislaus Lem's Solaris. Poe cycles Pym further south, to a great cataract, a white figure. What is it? God? In American Hieroglyphics, John T. Irwin argued that the figure Pym sees rising from this mist is his own shadow, a literal nonrecognition of his own shadow, concluding it is indeterminate precisely because it is overdetermined. Poe's perception of universal anxieties led him to Antarctica; the ice continues to make a perfect setting for weird human and nonhuman scenarios: Hollywood follows Poe's instincts, from The Thing, to Ice Station Zebra, to AVP: Alien vs. Predator. Science fiction warms to Antarctica, an otherworldly world right here on Earth.

Four

Like a Lorelei, Antarctica tempts men and then repels them, sounding a siren song of snow-filled wind, a wind that, as it sweeps over the haunted, crevassed wasteland, seems to shriek, like a Malraux character, "Death is always there, you understand, like a standing proof of the absurdity of life."

    —Jennie Darlington, *My Antarctic Honeymoon*

James Paton, posed with his daughters, one of whom was named Beaufort after the Antarctic island on which Paton was the first human to set foot.

James "Scotty" Paton had killed the penguin that met me when I walked into the Lyttelton Museum's Polar Gallery. Its weirdly thin neck reminded me that while some things are easy to master under the Antarctic's tough conditions, taxidermy was not one of them.

Baden Norris worked nearby, cleaning out display cases in the colonial New Zealand gallery. In addition to being the primary architect of how Antarctic histories were told in this and the Canterbury Museum, he also joined other volunteers in the day-to-day maintenance in Lyttelton. I asked about the penguin. "James Paton," Baden said, climbing down a small ladder, "was apparently a tough, cranky man; he placed his two young daughters in an orphanage when he found their mother—his wife—had made them eat boiled onions each night for dinner during his long absences, working on ships." Baden disappeared and returned with a brown tea tray. It was Wednesday and the museum was closed. We sat on Victorian-era high-backed, red-velvet chairs. Nearby, a mannequin sported World War I combat gear, complete with a postmodern fly-face gas mask. Someone had put a Santa hat on its head. Baden leaned forward and said, "Do you want to hear something really strange? Well, it's very hard to get mannequins for the museum displays. You know why? Some people collect them! Imagine that! Who would collect mannequins?"

I often could not tell if Baden was putting me on—could someone who collected bits of torn newspapers, half-eaten, hundred-year-old biscuits, both scavenged from Antarctic huts, find anyone else's collection strange? But such is the nature of obsession, I imagine. One's own feels so *right*.

He poured me a cup of tea. "What I want to tell you about is the life of Lyttelton as a, and perhaps *the*, crucial port of early Antarctic discovery. The whole town threw themselves into it! Schoolchildren raised money for the expeditions; Scott and Shackleton wandered these very streets. Many homes were decorated with penguins brought back by returning sailors! When the men came home to Lyttelton, they were heroes and they never had to buy another beer at the pub for the rest of their lives," Baden said.

"It sounds like Lyttelton was the Cape Canaveral for Antarctic exploration," I responded.

"Precisely," Baden laughed.

But all these stories of Antarctic voyages generated a lot of memorabilia that until late in the twentieth century was close to valueless. No one cared about these men or their things. No one had heard of Lyttelton. Yet as the century came to a close, early Antarctic histories caught on. A big Shackleton museum show and catalogue excited imaginations in America and the United Kingdom, rekindling interest in Antarctic heroes, spawning BBC documentaries, books, and films, including one starring Kenneth Branagh as Shackleton. Baden said the evolution of Antarctic awareness was remarkable—when visitors toured his two polar collections they came armed with a provisional expertise of Antarctic history. "Now our local boys take a place in the bigger picture—their stories fairly burst with bravery and often terrible sadness," he said. Baden poured more tea; in New Zealand, tea or coffee, and a biscuit, accompanies every conversation—after many months there, I was convinced that if cut, I would bleed tea.

Baden showed me a picture of Paton with the Antarctic ship Morning's crew. Paton wore the traditional flat-topped sailor's cap, rugged face set in a stern gaze. While I wouldn't say he was handsome, he had a face that a woman would be inclined to remember. You could see him staring down the rough, frigid Antarctic seas, smoking a small cigarette. He had a notable first to his credit, first man to step onto Beaufort Island in the Ross Sea, a small island north of Ross Island, home to the most continuous, extensive mosses in the McMurdo Sound region. He apparently scrambled across the ice to his prize. A peak there is named in his honor.

The Polar Gallery in Lyttelton requires time and care; you need to peer into the cases and slowly scrutinize rusted tins, sci-fi-ish snow blindness goggles, oats taken south to feed horses. Each shelf is comfortably packed with objects—"I would write myself a letter at Canterbury and ask if I could borrow something from the archives for Lyttelton. I usually said yes," Baden laughed.

A small, rather bad print caught my eye. I had never noticed it before, tucked beside biscuits swiped from huts built by Scott and his men. I had never seen anything like it.

Baden told me how after ships transported expeditions to Antarctica, they then turned around and came home to Lyttelton where the crew waited out the frigid, ship-crushing polar cold. Thus, Scott's second and final ship, the Terra Nova was moored at Lyttelton for long periods during 1910–1913. They

The Terra Nova *crew on parade in Lyttelton.*

would return in the spring thaw to fetch Scott and his victorious party, home from their dash to the South Pole. "The world was rapt with the South Pole race, and the Terra Nova and her crew were local celebrities," Baden added. You can imagine how people in Lyttelton would have felt, looking down into the port and seeing the Terra Nova in their midst.

Like many of her sailors, the Terra Nova simply vanished from history with her unlauded end coming during World War II, as she sank off the coast of Greenland, in the service of the U.S. Navy.

The photo captures a moment of pageant and freak show, P. T. Barnum does a wilderness act. Eleven men in Burberry anoraks, hoods extended and obscuring their faces. They wear harnesses and tow sledges just as five men will do en route to the South Pole. The first holds a crumpled Union Jack hastily hoisted on a pole. Two young boys gallop in from the right,

skinny legs, knee breeches and caps, white collars glistening. The street is caked in mud, the hillside homes cloaked in a faint coal-smoke haze. This is the end of the world and they are going further still. Behind the marchers, a regimental band, wearing topcoats with brass buttons. These Antarctic sailors march deliberately, suggesting they know where they are going—and in fact, they do—back to the quayside, a left turn and then two blocks down the steep hill, back to their ship's chores, then off to sea. Later, the photos will show these men at sea, faces masked by cold and ice, skin darkened and shining from coal and blubber smoke.

Some of these men were friends of Baden's and his father's. He often knew their children and spoke of them in a familiar manner, "oh, X's son was a detective in Christchurch. I must ring him and have him 'round for a cup of tea." Baden also recounted his findings in an Antarctic history column for the local paper. In one, whimsically titled "They Came Back to Lyttelton," he listed more than a dozen and their fates.

Baden is possessed with a distinctive elocution, slow, precise, his manner filled with modesty and mirth, and he is often in the Antarctic stories, a polar explorer himself, among other polar explorers, from men who sailed with Shackleton and Scott to Admiral Richard E. Byrd, the American naval aviator who pioneered Antarctic flight and is credited with getting the United States involved in Antarctic science and exploration. A walking Antarctic oral history, an ambulatory tape, an iPod set to ice stories, Baden generally refused to be taped or videotaped, which struck me as a profound loss. It was his insistence on the primacy of telling the stories rather than recording the stories that motivated me to write his take on history, and I also reflected, on more than one occasion, on how much Baden and Worsley shared an agency with Antarctic stories, how they stepped up over the years to remember, recollect, revise, order, and reflect. Reflection, a meditation or prayer, a spoken or unspoken communication with God, an ineluctable call to tell a story of place, to map a place with words, to make the unfathomable distance, the horizon, where Earth touches sky, real.

I never tired of listening to Baden's voice, resonant, slow, weaving in details of service medals, death, odd moments. Baden had mastered the well-rounded, quirky story as historical vehicle. He makes a specific statement in person as well: about five foot two, tan, bright blue eyes; some teeth in the back had gone missing, evident when he laughed, which was frequently.

"If you made it onto one of the Antarctic ships," Baden told me one day as we wandered the Lyttelton Museum, looking at ship's models, "you really were a significant cut above the rest."

I often wonder about those men. Were they obsessed with flight and distance, the blue of the sea? Did they cherish the moment their ship disappeared over the horizon? Many left school at eight or nine and so were functional illiterates and signed even their own names with a thumbprint on their seamen's tickets. Journals and letters of other simple seamen often were tossed because they were deemed without merit. Yet in some ways, their work reminded me of the raw energy seen in test pilots chronicled by Tom Wolfe. The right stuff—their skills channeled to a remarkable degree to make Scott and Shackleton's land journeys possible.

Baden grabbed fragments of these sailors lives and arranged them in the Lyttelton Museum, offering a collage, creating an abstraction, a verisimilitude of those working-class lives, the lives of sailors who called Lyttelton home between or before or after Antarctic trips. It seemed more decent this way, telling history as an open-ended series of images, words, a bright splash of blue, allowing each mind to grab and consider what the pieces might mean, what the past might be urging us to do with our lives now.

I looked at their black and white photos. Lance Corporal A. H. Blissett served aboard the Discovery, and by the time Baden knew him, he was Harry Blissett, a rather gruff watersider. "He frightened me as a child," he noted. Blissett was the first person in history to discover an intact emperor penguin's egg. (Scott recorded the moment in his diary on January 28, 1903: "all the news seems good. Blissett has discovered an Emperor penguin egg and his messmates expect him to be knighted." What's striking in this commentary is the almost rueful chortle, an aside, impecunious lower deck men.)

"Hugh McGowan served as an engineer with Shackleton's Nimrod, and continued that work back in Lyttelton. W. W. Knowles, an able-bodied seaman on the Terra Nova worked as a watersider on this very quayside. The Morning, a relief ship sent out in 1903 [and in an odd moment of language meeting purpose, mourning, the feeling of showing deep sadness following the death of somebody, they sailed south] to find and bring home Scott and his Discovery crew when they were late returning, had two Lyttelton men aboard; Arthur Beaumont, able-bodied seaman, who worked in Lyttelton as a watersider and crane operator, and Jack Partridge, who sailed with the Morning and then headed south again in 1907 on Shackleton's Nimrod. He became fireman on the Lyttelton Harbour Board's dredge Te Whaka." Baden took a breath. "Not all the Lyttelton men were sailors. Local boy Eric Norman Webb," Baden pointed out, "a mere 22 when selected by the now-legendary Australian polar scientist and explorer Douglas Mawson to head south."

Webb served as chief magnetician with the 1911 Australasian Expedition, key in locating the South Magnetic Pole. (The magnetic poles, or geocentric dipoles, describe for the Earth's magnetic field the equivalent of the geographic poles. The South Magnetic Pole is not fixed and drifts like a cloud across water, land, ice. When last I checked, it hovered over the Southern Ocean, not far off the Antarctic coastline.) Webb went on to become a world authority on hydroelectric power.

Men connected by place. Antarctica roping them all together in a tiny town hanging off the edge of the Earth, a town as vibrant with firsthand discovery, eyewitnesses, and idea as . . . where? Paris? Cambridge? Tokyo? Imagine the conversations in those pubs. (Again, the test pilots to astronauts came to mind, first at a motel in the desert, drinking and telling stories about trying to break the sound barrier, then sitting beside President John F. Kennedy.) I saw these Lyttelton men scouring the ground, looking for clues, like children on their hands and knees, climbing ropes, jumping across ice floes, stopping to bag the occasional penguin. The Antarctic far from an abstract concept. A place.

The phone in the museum rang, the strange sonorous ring of a 1970s telephone. I had seen it on the wall: harvest gold with a long cord so the talker could walk into a closet for some privacy. Baden answered it. A television team from the United Kingdom wanted to schedule time around the harbor for the comedian and actor Billy Connelly. They wanted Baden to serve as tour guide and appear on Connelly's show, which featured him traveling the world, checking out exotic places. I waved good-bye. Walking back to my cottage on the other side of town, I climbed cement stairs through the Baden Norris gardens, turned and gazed out across the deep turquoise water to Diamond Harbour on the other shore. A bay cruise boat, black and white, pulled slowly away from the quay, a dolphin-watching trip, but earlier in the year a pod of orcas made the unusual move of swimming into the harbor and gobbling up a lot of the tiny, rare Hector's dolphins that also called Lyttelton home. Those that remained kept a low profile and no one had seen any in months.

The next morning, I had a coffee at the Number Six café on London Street and observed how similar Lyttelton's main street looked to that in the parade photograph—so little had changed. I returned to the Lyttelton Museum but Baden was off to Christchurch.

The Lyttelton Museum faced the port along Gladstone Quay, and the heavy doors pushed open to reveal an entrance hall filled with photos, statues, and a long, rising staircase. I climbed the stairs to the second-floor Polar Gallery, with its black-and-white-tile checkerboard floor and mint-green walls. My eyes came to rest on a collection of sepia-toned photographs, one hand labeled "Southward Bound" in white

Polar clothes modeled by donated department-store mannequins at the Lyttelton Museum. Note how the model on the right, accustomed to showing the latest fall fashions, vigilantly searches the horizon in her new role.

ink on a black mat. It was one of Ponting's famed images and shows Scott and a dozen men on Ross Island. The *Terra Nova* was depicted in Lyttelton, tied up where the *Greenpeace* had undergone engine repairs. Framed newspaper accounts announced, "The Polar Disaster," and showed Scott and his men not as polar explorers and naval officers, but as ordinary middle-class men in vested suits. A raised white platform dominated the room, on which perched a stuffed penguin, roughly three feet in height. A New Zealand flag hung from the wall, a facsimile of one made by Lyttelton District High School students to raise money for Scott. White block letters stitched on blue read, "L.D.H.S. to Terra Nova 1910."

A long glass case displayed a silver setting engraved with the Terra Nova expedition logo—they had china and stemware to match—next to rusted pony-shoe nails from Shackleton's expeditions, a sealskin watch strap bearing Antarctic relics from the Terra Nova, made by the Lyttelton polar sailor Mortimer McCarthy, and a large map, circa 1915 labeled "The Toll of the Antarctic: Where Captain Scott and his comrades met their doom." The Lyttelton Polar Gallery is a rectangular room originally built to house a billiards table, on the second floor of the former seaman's mission, originally built to get hard-drinking long-haul seamen off the town's streets. Paton's badly stuffed emperor penguin craned its neck, watching a group of mannequins forever laboring on a white-painted stage. The four wore authentic polar field clothes donated by New Zealand, American, and Japanese Antarctic programs, fur-trimmed hoods pulled over faces, mouths a pale peach, eyes painted with heavy black eyeliner. Before they set off for their polar mission, these mannequins were accustomed to standing in store windows, modeling the season's fashions.

I looked at the four, their distant stare was actually somewhat similar to what you see in photographs of actual Antarctic explorers, particularly the men who got lost, ran out of food and fuel, or watched a mate dangle helplessly down a crevasse. They had the look of people who did not need to be asked if the Antarctic had changed their lives. Perhaps a more realistic depiction than some would have guessed.

On one wall, over a bench donated from the Terra Nova, the stuffed head of a sledge dog named Deek, a silver Siberian Samoyed, gazed off into the distance with cold blue-

Deek's head, stuffed and mounted, on display in the Lyttelton Museum. To his right, a commercially produced portrait of his master, Robert Falcon Scott.

glass eyes. Deek traveled to Antarctica with Scott in 1910, but unlike his master, managed to make it back to warmer climes alive. Christchurch's mayor received Deek as a present for the townspeople's help to the expedition.

When he died, they decided to memorialize his polar work by mounting his head, which struck me as a practical choice: A head was much easier to work into one's décor. A whole dog almost needed a special atrium created simply for his mildewing pelt. The specific irony of Deek's reign was that while master froze and starved in no small part because he refused to use dogs to pull his sledges, famously choosing instead the backs of men, this dog made it home safely. To the dog's right was a black and white photo of Scott and his men before they set out, science-fictionesque, Inuit inspired goggles and fur mitts dangling, faces shiny with sunburn. They stand in a line up with Mount Erebus as backdrop.

The musty Lyttelton Polar Gallery offered Antarctic rocks next to rusting tins of Coleman's mustard, next to worn, cinnamon-colored felt hats, all joined by their association with Antarctica, with the viewers' imagination deployed to link it all together, behind the objects, the faces of men who dared to conquer the Antarctic. Paton's dour face stared out at me, Paton who rarely appears in canonical Antarctic accounts— a man who made a remarkable nine trips to the Ross Sea in the early twentieth century. Leslie B. Quartermain, a New Zealand Antarctic historian, wrote,

> the Aurora complement now included two New Zealanders, C. P. La Motte, Chief Officer, and Bos'n Paton, a Lyttelton man who had previously served on the Morning, Nimrod, and Terra Nova, in the Antarctic, a unique record. Davis [the captain of the Aurora], responded that it would be "difficult to overrate the value of his [Paton's] experience and common-sense in a voyage of this kind."

If you look at Antarctic exploration before 1930, the number of men traveling there specifically to explore was minuscule—between 1901 and 1922, five or so ships sailed to the Ross Sea, Discovery, Morning, Nimrod, Terra Nova, Aurora, Kainan Maru, all with crews of thirty or so men, half of whom were scientists and officers, half of whom were specialized Antarctic crews Baden calls simple seamen.

Colonial Life in Lyttelton came to life across the hall from the Polar collections. Mannequins, dressed in drab calico skirts, arranged around a cradle draped in lace and holding a doll resembling a child from a Roman Polanski film, the room had shiny chocolate brown linoleum floors and fifteen-foot ceilings lined with elaborate wainscoting, and was packed with dusty cases. I brushed aside some dead silverfish. An emu egg, bits of clay pipes salvaged from the

Lyttelton dump in the late 1800s, a metal curling iron that looked like a tuning fork, a ticket from the Oddfellows' Jubilee Banquet December 20, 1901, a metal bank fashioned to look like the post office, a glass razor holder. Each piece was carefully identified in neat calligraphic handwriting. In the corner, a dark wood pipe organ with a sign that requested you not sit down and play. The organ, I later learned, came from a church further around the harbor, where Scott and his Terra Nova crew had their last, earthly mass. The church fell into disrepair and Baden insisted he wanted to preserve the organ as part of the Antarcticana collection, hence its salvation from the scrap heap. It was the last organ those men heard, he said, winking at me.

Back in the Polar Gallery, Charlie Williams gazed down at me from above the doors. A small card told his story: Born in Lyttelton in 1881, he was a decorated hero of World War I—fighting on the HMS Broke alongside his famed former shipmate, the noted Antarctic explorer Lieutenant E. R. G. R. Evans (Cape Evans), later Lord Mountevans. He had made three trips to Antarctica on the Terra Nova, in 1910–1912, received the Polar Medal, and wound up back in Lyttelton working at sea—on a wooden fuel ship, humping petrol up and down the New Zealand coast. It was dangerous work and all hands save one were lost in 1919 when the ship caught fire and blew to smithereens, a brief and brilliant blaze.

Each voyage represented an avalanche of new ideas, used gear, discoveries. Can we imagine what it must have felt like, a mysterious new continent unfolding in a parade of objects, each one a trigger for stories, stories told by men who lined the local pubs? Stories they told in the first person because they had been there. The room's contents recorded a landscape's journey into the minds and homes and museum collections of women and men who might never go there, people who would find themselves on a Sunday morning gazing thoughtfully at a bracelet fashioned from crabeater seal teeth, fastened onto a thick, gold band, made from teeth brought home to New Zealand by an Antarctic sailor.

The geological story of Lyttelton was told in a hallway case adjacent to steep stairs. Each rock labeled on shiny gold paper, the sort with hologram-like metallic prisms that shimmer in the light. When Scott and Shackleton went to Antarctica, public museums of natural history were coming into their own.

> *The museum of natural history is the depository for objects which illustrate the forces and phenomena of nature—the named units included within the three kingdoms, animal, vegetable, and mineral,—and whatever illustrates their origin in time (or phylogeny), their individual origin, development, growth, function, structure, and geographical distribution, past and present: also their relation to each other, and their influence upon the structure of the earth and phenomena observed upon it!*

Written by G. Brown Goode (and quoted in The Birth of the Museum by Tony Bennett) in 1895, The Principles of Museum Administration represents the ideal surrounding exploration in the late nineteenth and into the early twentieth century: Explorers set out for the unknown charged with collecting samples—including humans—for edification of the masses on their return. Stories of Antarctic voyages had to fulfill this obligation.

I paused in the hall, reading the handwritten cards telling the stories of Lyttelton's natural history.

> *Like grotesque giants eroded relics of rhyolite are reminders of an ancient volcanic field predating the main formation of Akaroa and Lyttelton volcanoes. These rhyolite and andesitic rocks were produced by more explosive eruptions 90 million years ago.*

In the case, on small cards described in shaky, black calligraphy:

> *volcanic glass, lithophysue, syenite, basalt, red ash, hawaiite basalt, loess wind-blown "rock flour," pitchstone, perlite, devitrified volcanic rhyolite glass, spherulitic rhyolite, quartz-speckled rhyolite, obsidian.*

Mr. Goode would be pleased, I imagined, recalling his prescriptive words.

This case stood adjacent to the front desk, a half-door topped by a wide counter, above which hung a sign, "Floggings will stop when morale improves." On the counter, one of New Zealand's indigenous penguins, a little blue, watched the front door with glass eyes. I stepped into the bright sunlight, and stood for a moment next to a line of eighteen Filipino fishermen in guts-spattered white and orange jumpsuits, waiting to use the pay phone. The karaoke club next door thumped out "I Will Survive."

I closed my eyes and imagined life at the turn of the twentieth century. In 1901 Robert Falcon Scott's ship Discovery sailed to this same quayside. She was bound for the Antarctic, the first of Scott's two attempts to reach the pole. Her crew list reads like an Antarctic all-star roster: Lieutenant Ernest Shackleton; his fellow Irishman Tom Crean (the only man to sail with every major British expedition during the two decades of the Heroic Age and who would later make the small boat journey with Worsley); Albert Armitage (who had spent three years in the Arctic with the Jackson-Harmsworth expedition and recommended Shackleton to Scott); Edward Wilson, a naturalist, mystic, and doctor who would later die with Scott returning from the pole; and Louis Bernacchi, a physicist who had been among the first men to winter in the Antarctic, under the command of Carsten Borchegrevink at Cape Adare.

For New Zealanders, the arrival of Discovery on November 28, 1901, signaled a new role for their geographically isolated society. (The British expeditions of this period headed for the Ross Sea all followed a similar path. After an initial departure from London, they would sail the Atlantic, round the Cape of Good Hope, call in at South Africa, then on to New Zealand.) They took over the town of Lyttelton and its harbor and then into Christchurch. *When famous people come to town.* It's not that there were so many, it's that what they planned to do blew every other person and activity out of the room with the sheer force of its imagination and intensity. Even their dogs carried a similar awe-inspiring aura —the island where they were quarantined, in the middle of the harbor, now offers a restored dog kennel as historic site. You take a boat across the blue water and then hike to a long-abandoned, then carefully restored dog kennel.

You see it again and again, how the new world was realized in the books of these explorers, how the world was mapped in a new way, how their mighty blue-sea voyages over the horizon to the ice began and ended in Lyttelton, a coal-blackened, hastily thrown-together colonial port, the white-hot center of the biggest game going: South Pole conquest. The race for the South Pole had begun.

A summer dinner in downtown Christchurch at a French Moroccan place, Simo's. Nick Lambourn, who handled travel-related and polar objects for Christie's auctions in London, was in New Zealand seeking items for sale. Lambourn explained how he placed ads in local papers and then people brought their Antarctic treasures to his hotel to have them appraised. Baden Norris and Kerry McCarthy, the Canterbury Museum photo curator, had organized the dinner, and we all

Field Notes

sat around a large round table eating trays of grilled eggplant, rice with almonds and apricots, and shrimp cooked and served in a graceful terra-cotta tagine.

Lambourn told a story of how Peter Scott's widow (Peter was the explorer Scott's only child) opened a leather suitcase, embossed with PS, revealing RFS memorabilia and gear—including goggles worn on the final South Pole journey.

Baden wanted to know what happened to it all.

We sold it, Lambourn said, taking a sip of his Chardonnay.

Everyone laughed.

Over the course of the meal Lambourn told us how the polar auction market had slowed and he did not see a market developing for more contemporary relics—such as things from Byrd's expeditions during the 1930s. There's no interest in the United States at present for it, he said. In 2000 Christie's had sold blue prints and other plans to Scott's ship Discovery for an amazing 163,000 British pounds against the presale estimate of 20,000–30,000 pounds. The market for Heroic Age relics had threatened to heat to a point where museums could no longer compete. During the past four years Christie's had organized more than a dozen polar auctions around the world: paintings, spoons, hats, medals, journals, books.

Lambourn asked what my book was about, and I said, Lyttelton and Christchurch, their relationship with the Antarctic, and how people tell their stories of a place very, very few people will ever visit.

Lambourn looked at me and said, deadpan, "Places most people will never visit, like Lyttelton and Christchurch?"

Five

The love of wilderness is more than a hunger for what is always beyond reach; it is also an expression of loyalty to the earth, the earth which bore us and sustains us, the only paradise we shall ever know, the only paradise we ever need—if only we had the eyes to see.

— Edward Abbey, *Desert Solitaire*

Driving into town from Lyttelton (as Lytteltonians say when going to Christchurch), cars and huge trucks bearing timber from the west coast zoom through a beige, shiny-tiled tunnel, cut through steep hills descending to the Canterbury Plain, also called the Big Flat, the largest stretch of flat land in New Zealand, then into Christchurch, the commercial and artistic center of the South Island. The hills ringing the port create a natural barrier—the historically working-class town from the South Island's largest metropolitan area. This was my path when I had to wrest myself from my home on the tonic slopes of Lyttelton to glue my eyeballs to archival documents. Lyttelton, where I had first lived in 1988, however, while it looked largely unchanged, indeed was slowly absorbing a new wave of immigrants, people taken by the rare views offered by the line of eroding giant volcano against blue sky. People bearing money to transform empty storefronts into wine bars offering goat cheese spread on grilled bread, pan-seared gurnard, and warm chocolate gateau creating a Lyttelton proffered as destination and object, a place to observe and take in and consider rather than a place to work, to unload ships, to drink handles of beer held in rough working-men's and-women's hands.

Baden had phoned to tell me about a letter penned by James Paton, written from Antarctica while he served aboard *Terra Nova*. The letter, Baden said, demonstrated the particular insights lower-deck men offered as reporters of simple fact.

It also represented the working seaman's perspective, notably absent from most museum accounts of Antarctic exploration. Cultural memory and historical erasure, things that aren't monumented and how we don't remember them. There is no monument anywhere in the world listing the names of all the sailors who traveled to Antarctica. Why do I think there should be? Would those men really care? Why do I? Why does it bother me so much that they are being ground up under the tractor treads of history? Sometimes my research into their lives came to a dead end and I had to find another way forward. My colleague in polar histories, the Canterbury Museum photography curator Kerry McCarthy suggested that photographs—they all owned cameras—offered the best record of working class people. Image telling a story words missed. I studied their faces, their rough boots, rakish hats, strong forearms crossed over muscular chests. They looked directly at the camera and posed with an ease and poise often absent from the "hero construction" set pieces of Antarctic leaders' photos.

In many photos the men are not even identified beyond "crew." In order to inscribe and reinscribe their names someone had to write them all down, to create some sort of monument first in words and so James Paton steps onto the stage.

Today as Christchurch-bound cars disappeared into the auto tunnel, the landscape blurred and waving, I thought of

the tunnel builders' determined work. The railway tunnel
was completed in 1867, a noted feat of engineering and particularly ambitious for a group of people living in a colonial
backwater—it was also the first tunnel in the world bored
through an extinct volcano.

In 1903 Paton was a sailor on the *Morning*, a ship that served as
a resupply vessel for Antarctic expeditions. For a period during the austral summer of 1903, three ships and their crews
were within sight of one another in the Ross Sea—a traffic
jam of ships, the *Discovery*, the *Morning*, and the *Aurora*. Not
just any sailor was chosen as crew for an Antarctic voyage.
Rather than mindless drones working behind the scenes, the
sailors offered a visceral fragmented narrative, a collage of
raw life on Antarctic ships. Their stories added texture to a
sea of smooth, glossed accounts. Unlike their leaders, they
wrote without guile. Their absence from history reflected
class conceit and snobbery and a disinterest in the very fact
of exploration itself. I eased into the carpark at Hagley Park,
watched for a moment as two local college boys tossed a rugby
ball back and forth, advancing, cutting, running.

I met Baden in the glassed-in portion of the Canterbury
Museum Archives, and we set to work.

What struck me initially in Paton's handwritten account,
a letter home to a sweetheart, was his fine penmanship. In
1903 he recorded both tense days of trying to extricate the
Discovery trapped in the ice before they finally succeeded, as
well as how he and others helped the scientists. His journal is titled "Rough Log of the Morning from Hobart to the
Antarctic Circle and Back." Paton wrote, "Twelve months
ago today we spent our Xmas in about the same place as we
are now, but such a vast difference last Christmas morn we
had a bright burning Sun shining over us, but this one we
cannot see the sun for fog." On January 24 the *Discovery* was
still beset in the ice and he wrote, "After tea, Jack Pepper

and I went on shore for a run, visited Doctor Wilson's camp, assisted him to pull on shore a large sea elephant, a new specimen of an Animal which never was known to exist in these regions, got on board about midnight bringing some birds' eggs and granite."

(I later asked my former shipmate and friend the Antarctic navigator Robert Graham how Paton could manage this while at sea. "You wait until she's not throwing you all over the bloody place," he remarked dryly.) Paton used the official *Terra Nova* stationery—a logo of emperor penguin perched on a globe, ringed by the words "British Antarctic Expedition, *Terra Nova* RYS." The penguin stands in profile, gazing steadfastly to the right. Baden and I sat, as we often did, side by side at the long table in the glass-enclosed room in the archives. I read aloud in a hushed tone to Baden, who was seated to my right, logging glass lantern slides.

I held Paton's letter in white cotton–gloved hands. It begins:

> CHRISTMAS 1910
> Knowing only too well how little time we shall have on hand when we get to our destination I think I had better begin my letters now. We left Port Chalmers at 2.30 P.M. on November 29th, and all went well until December 2nd when we ran into a heavy southerly gale our decks were heavily laden with cargo. Beside having 3 large moter [sic] sledges and all the cases of petrel for this use, upwards of 250 bags of coal had been put on board at Port Chalmers besides bales of hay, timber and numerous other things.

"Keep in mind that this was someone who knew the sea and would be fairly confident in his skills," Baden commented, squinting at the slides through a magnifying glass, not looking up from his task.

I continued reading:

> A heavy sea was running and our decks were constantly awash heavy seas breaking on board putting our fires out, tearing our deck cargo from its lashings, washing away a great part of our Port Bulwarks, we were left tumbling about at the mercy of the wind and sea, with no more sail than our Main Lower Topsail, the deck cargo washing from one side of the deck to the other and to save the ship was well as our own lives we had to turn too and throw a good part of the deck cargo overboard, this was not our only danger, as it soon leeked [sic] out that the water had risen as high as the bottom of our furnaces, the continental wash of the water in the hold carried the small coal through into the wells kept choking the pumps so that for 48 hours all hands were employed all the time up to the waist in water, with the seas breaking over them while the aftergaurd [sic] (the officers and scientists) were kept passing it from the Engine room in buckets.

It was an inauspicious beginning for men who hoped to be first to the South Pole. I considered how Scott must have felt, watching it all, head fully locked onto the walking/skiing journey to the South Pole. Men without fanfare who took leaking, wooden ships into and out of the Antarctic were singular heroes.

> All this time we had very little to eat (nothing hot) and no rest, and for our own sakes as well as for the poor dumb animals we had on board, it was a relief the weather moderated.
>
> During this gale we had one dog washed overboard, and two of our horses got down and died but several days passed before we could get them out of the stalls to throw them overboard.
>
> From this till we entered the ice on the 9th December we had an excellent weather and everything looked as if it was in our favour but we encountered very heavy Field Ice and up to the

present we have scarcely made more than 100 miles, for days at a stretch we have been completely frozen in and all hands been out on the Ice practisering [sic] to walk on Ski.

Paton never complains nor reveals that he finds the whole endeavor ghastly. Life at sea is a hard life. Or maybe he was simply a brave man of character. Scott, on the other hand, famously wrote about the South Pole, "Great God! This is an awful place . . ."

In fact, Paton reports a view of the eternal now:

> *We have also had sledges and dogs out for training and at intervals broke the monotony by excercising [sic] ourselves by playing football Men versus Officers, At other times we would find after days steaming we were no further than 2½ miles ahead so at last Capt. Scott decided on having the fires drawn to save coal and depend on the sailing qualities of the ship to get through when the ice opens. So here we are and although we are today jammed hard and fast in the ice, it is not safe to go any distance away from the Ship.*
>
> *On the whole we are having a very fair Xmas, have had some presents from Dunedin, from Captain Scott each man received a Box of Cigars, Whisky, Wine, Stout, Cake, Sweets, and Plum puddings in Galore of what was provided for the inner man I will leave you to guess for yourself, I am perfectly satisfied with the food supplied in our every day life, and do not admire a glutton, as I would rather not write about it.*

I considered Paton's words: Imagine what he does not, will not say. He will not say that among the sailors there are but one or two who are literate. That when they signed on for Antarctica they had their bodies inspected like cattle and among their compromises to their new masters was submission to preemptive tooth removal, that is, the crude ripping of tooth from gums, tooth that may or may not become a source of pain and lost man hours while in the Antarctic. I hear the commands, open your mouth please. *Well, this one will have to come out.*

I read the list of Christmas presents aloud again to Baden: "Cigars, Whisky, Wine, Stout, Cake, Sweets, and Plum puddings." It sounded like some fruit basket prepared in advance by the catering team at Claridge's. "Scott was so out of touch with the men on the ship," I half mumbled.

"I know I've seen some sailor—it will come to me—commenting on the fact he never saw Scott the entire time he worked on the *Terra Nova*," Baden said. "She wasn't a large ship; it speaks to the separation enforced, officers and scientists in one realm, ship's personnel in another."

"That makes Scott sound like Ahab," I said. "What do you think he was getting at when he says he leaves it to her to guess herself about what was provided for the inner man . . ."

Baden put down the magnifying glass. "Dunno. Church services? Most likely something about faith and hope and salvation."

I turned my eyes back to the pages. Paton wrapped up his thoughts:

> Now as I have given you a Very fair account of the passage up to date I will close for the remainder of this year, we are only awaiting a chance to breakthrough and resume our journey when the ice opens, it seems to be on the move now, and who knows but before the year is out yet we may be well down towards our destination.

Paton resumes this correspondence with the startling realization they are not alone:

> But here to our surprise we found the Norwegian Explorer Amundsen with Nanson's old ship the Fram. He almost had his winter quarters built was preparing for a dash for the Pole,

The ship Aurora, masts so many crosses, in the Ross Sea pack ice. Even today small pieces of floating ice, like that in the foreground, can punch a hole in a ship.

> he has 122 dogs for the Purpose and is determined to give Capt Scott a hard run for it.
> We immediately went back to McMurdo Sound and left word for Capt. Scott warning him of the danger.

The danger of losing the race, of finding his strange daydream not singular, instead a duplication of another, bolder dream held by the esteemed Amundsen. The race to the pole was not about getting there; it was about getting there first, getting the flag hoisted onto the bamboo, and bringing back the photos for all to see.

Another folder lay on the table. In it, Paton and two well-coiffed young women. The caption identified them as his daughters, one of whom he named Beau, for Beaufort Island, Antarctica—a piece of ice and rock in the Ross Sea; Paton was the first man to ever step on its shores. What, I wondered, had happened to my storytelling sailor mate? I wanted to read more of his life at sea.

When the Antarctic work finished—Scott dead, ships sold, men dispersed—Paton took a job with another ship that had done Antarctic work, the *Aurora*. The *Aurora* was a Scottish-built barquentine, one funnel and three masts, with a bow of solid wood reinforced with steel-plate armor. Originally designed as a sealer, she worked in Antarctica from 1911 to 1916 ferrying supplies and aid to the most famed Ross Sea expeditions. In 1917 the *Aurora* and Paton sailed from Newcastle, New South Wales, coal-laden, bound for Chile, and mysteriously vanished in the Pacific.

Baden explained, "There are two theories. Either she hit a mine left from the war, or something in the cargo hold caught fire and she blew to bits. At any rate it was fast and thorough." When he died at sea, Paton had been to the Antarctic a breathtaking nine times. (Paton was awarded the Silver Polar Medal—a higher honor than the Bronze—and subsequently earned two additional silver bars recognizing his Antarctic service on the *Terra Nova* and the *Aurora*, which supported Shackleton's Ross Sea Party. In their recommendations following the Shackleton expedition, the Hydrographer's Office in London noted in the official record that while crew usually received the lesser of the two Polar Medals—bronze—because they were merely carrying out routine duties not connected with scientific exploration, in the case of the *Aurora*'s crew [on Antarctic resupply missions], although certain members of the party remained on board the ship and may therefore be described as carrying out transport work, these duties were carried out under most exceptional circumstances . . .)

Baden stacked folders back into green boxes as the Canterbury archives closed for the afternoon. They were open a meager three hours a day. I peeled off the thin white cotton gloves, sad to leave behind the letters and diaries, disinterested in returning to what seemed to be a wholly mundane

The Aurora crew on deck. Note supplies in wooden crates lashed to the rails. Heavy seas often swept supplies and coal overboard during the rough passage south.

world in contrast. I would go home to Lyttelton and drink coffee at the No. 6 Café on London Street and imagine the sidewalks filled with Antarctic sailors, ready to sit down and yarn. To many eyes, Lyttelton looked like a dingy port town, slowly being gentrified and overrun with what Baden catalogued as television people and artists. To my Antarctican eyes, the sagging shop fronts were animated with the stories of those exciting days—when the world whispered, "Come look at my wonders," and men sought it in small, leaky wooden boats. Far too few of us heard that call anymore.

⋆　⋆　⋆

We wandered out to the museum's Polar Gallery. A group of ten-and eleven-year-old schoolchildren in blue-gingham smocks, kilts, and blazers giggled and pointed at the life-size dioramas of stuffed huskies at work in Antarctica. Baden stopped to talk with them, and pointed out that sledge dogs made long Antarctic hauls practical, possible, and survivable.

"Who made the dogs like this?" a red-haired boy called out before being shushed by his teacher.

Baden began, "This was my idea and it is the only one of its kind in the world, although I do know of a library in Australia where a stuffed team in harness races towards the stacks."

The dogs were one of a series of dioramas, tranquil true-to-life stuffed penguins and seals, staged against vast, hand-painted murals depicting Antarctic skies, pale lavender, teal, celadon, smoky clouds, scenes of Mount Erebus, thin lines of lemon light, and underfoot sparkling white "ice." Emperor penguins stood attentively within this paperboard wilderness.

In the dog diorama, a reddish husky jumped up to greet a well-bundled man in front of a replica of New Zealand's Scott Base on Ross Island—the dog on hind legs, resting front paws on the man's chest, happy to see him after a day in the field. Another shaggy husky stood nearby, watching the horizon.

Baden animated the two huskies' lives. When the red-headed boy said he found the dogs nasty looking, Baden reminded the children that without dogs, the Antarctic could not have been explored. They are often-overlooked heroes of early exploration.

He continued, "Horses, motorized sledges, men's own backs—none could compare to a team of well-trained dogs for speed and success of mission. In addition, the dogs offered Antarctic travelers a welcome break from the deadening ice landscape; curled in blizzard-weathering balls, yelping and lunging at penguins, yoked and ready to pull across the white, they offered a tireless message: Let's get going."

By the 1960s dog teams had been largely replaced by motorized vehicles, except for deep fieldwork. The Antarctic Treaty nations agreed in 1994 that dogs posed potential risk to native species—penguins and seals—from distemper and other introduced diseases—and they were banned from Antarctica.

The children sat in silence, mouths agape, alternately

looking between Baden—his silver-hair shining under the overhead light—and the silvered, bear-like dogs, the larger of the two weighing well over a hundred pounds, posed behind the glass.

He told them a story. One Antarctic summer season, Baden worked cleaning up and cataloguing one of Scott's huts. Ice migrated into and inhabited the huts, locking everything from hams to paper in a cold storage, and Baden's job was to clear it out. He had to tackle a number of problems, from preserving handwritten diaries frozen into ice to strengthening collapsing roofs, and extreme care was needed with each swing of the pick to spare damage to artifacts.

On these trips, his keen eye searched out fragments and scraps, often yielding the rare and overlooked; one find was a theatrical written and performed in early twentieth-century Antarctica, the pages of which had been shredded in places for cigarette papers and toilet tissue. The children tittered.

Baden recalled how he set out from base for his task each morning at eight and returned each afternoon at four; one day, when walking back for dinner, a large, rusty pup bounded across the snow to meet him. The pup's name was Jens, and from then on Jens slid and ran over blue ice to greet him each day.

However, Baden intoned, "you really shouldn't make friends with sledge dogs; they need to be treated with supreme discipline, to be hardened to the cold and the tough conditions. It was their only hope for survival when caught in the inevitable screaming wind and cold. They aren't pets."

Yet Baden kept tabs on the pup over the years; he grew to be an enormous dog and leader of teams. When Jens died in 1977 after a long life in Antarctica, Baden heard of and mourned his passing. Many months later, he received word that a dog skin was available for the museum. Baden had long wanted to honor the dogs of Antarctica with a museum display. Without seeing it, he had the skin shipped to a master taxidermist with the request to make the dog appear lifelike. Then, one wintry morning, a deliveryman arrived at the museum, asking Baden to sign for a large wooden crate. As their crowbars cracked into the crate, sawdust floated into the air and Jens emerged before him. The taxidermist, of course, had no idea that this dog once chased Baden across Ross Island. The dog arrived posed on his hind legs, with his two forepaws ready to rest on a man's chest. So. A man and his dog reunited.

I listened and looked at the dog and man under glass, Baden's voice rich, never wavering nor losing enthusiasm, it struck me as I peered at the dog diorama, that the man in the case was Baden—bearded, knit cap pulled onto forehead, but undoubtedly the same nose and clear blue eyes. *Crikey.* So you get to know the stories, and the men and the dogs and you step into the Antarctic landscape, a looking glass, an ice mirror, and, like Alice, you become the museum.

From James Paton's 1903 diary, written on board the Morning, while in Antarctica (inscribed on the title page: "James Paton, Sumner Road, Lyttelton"):

As today is the first anniversary of my youngest daughter's birth and she being in many ways connected with the expedition her father being an A.B. her Godfather second officer and her uncle a fireman on board the Morning and she herself named after the furthest Island South, she is certainly worthy of mention on this day at least. I sincerely hope and trust that she may be spared to read in history of what has been done in the past two years and that she as well as the world in general may benefit thereof.

Field Notes

Six

A conviction of the fundamental soundness of the idea took root in my mind.

—Alfred Wegener

Wegener's hypothesis in general is of the foot-loose type, in that it takes considerable liberty with our globe, and is less bound by restrictions or tied down by awkward, ugly facts than most of its rivals. Its appeal seems to lie in the fact that it plays a game in which there are few restrictive rules and no sharply drawn code of conduct.

— R. T. Chamberlain, esteemed American geologist, University of Chicago

. . . utter damned rot!

—W. B. Scott, former president of the American Philosophical Society, expressing the prevalent American view of his day on the notion that continents could "drift"

I slept curled in a rectangle of white light, watched by the bellbirds and gulls flying in a wide, clear Lyttelton sky. I had dozed off 180 million years ago, in the deep time of geologic stories, the rocks underfoot and towering above slipping in the idea that our minute-by-minute, day-by-day take on things was not entirely fair and accurate reporting. As I shook off sleep, the open text offered a photo of the German meteorologist and geophysicist Alfred Wegener. In 1912, while Scott and Amundsen raced to the South Pole, Wegener published his own discoveries: *Die Entstehung der Kontinente und Ozeane*, in English, *The Origin of Continents and Oceans*.

Wegener's "utter damned rot" ideas became the dominant geologic story by the mid-twentieth century. A tall, trim, gray-bearded Irishman named Bryan Storey, a geologist who directed Gateway Antarctica National Research Centre in Christchurch, was teaching all of this to me. Gateway hosted polar researchers from around the world; during my Fulbright tenure I was one of them. My colleagues included

Alan Hemmings, a silver-haired English scientist and legal scholar engaged in research on environmental issues and the Antarctic Treaty; Gary Steele, a Canadian psychologist who studied how people dealt with extreme environments and capsule living; and Luke Copeland, a Cambridge-trained glaciologist who worked in both the Arctic and the Antarctic—he was studying the Ross Ice Shelf, placing sensors in the ice and monitoring it for early stresses associated with global warming. When I first met Luke he shook my hand, smiled, and said, "I am bipolar. I research ice in both the Antarctic and Arctic."

Across the hall, Michelle Finnemore, an American-born New Zealand transplant, managed all of Gateway's programs, students, publications, and staff. Further down the hall, Paul Barr, the global positioning system technician, duplicated Antarctic maps from Gateway's prodigious collection for research groups around the world; next door to him was an Australian mapmaker named Yvonne Cooke.

A walk down the corridor—lined with blue and green watercolors created on the ice, as well as poster presentations from recent international meetings (taxonomy and ecology of Antarctic algae)—for coffee often invited wonderful, off-the-cuff reflections on Antarctican lives. All of us had lived in the Antarctic for months, some for years. During one of these chats, Alan offered me a most-gripping contemporary Antarctic story. From April to mid-June 1982, the Falklands conflict raged—Argentina launched a surprise invasion on the U.K.-controlled islands—the region's only war. Alan managed the British Antarctic Survey's remote Signy Island station (in the vicinity of the Falklands) during this time, and one afternoon he received a radio message from a Royal Navy ship with the order to relay it to the garrison of eighty Royal Marines stationed in the Falklands. The simple message directed: If attacked by the Argentines, the garrison in the Falklands was to return fire. I wondered how the soldiers reacted, sitting at their remote camp, on a windswept island populated by about one thousand people, when he rang with that message. "No reaction, just an acknowledgment that they had received the order," he said.

I spent many days culling the scientific and political subtext of Antarctica, an essential piece of the landscape's syntax, essential to understanding Antarctica. The continent evolved into a giant geopolitical experiment, effectively ruled by scientific agendas. It seemed that one interpretation of Wegener's ideas could be that they propelled expeditions throughout most of the twentieth century—geology in the early twentieth century was among the hottest areas of inquiry, in no small part because refined methods—like the chemical dating of rocks—made it clear the Earth was much older than what the Bible stated.

Wegener's radical argument offered this simple conclusion: Continents drift across the Earth's surface. Furthermore, they had once been one massive continent, which Wegener called Pangaea, pan meaning all, and gaea meaning Earth. Wegener saw the Earth as a great collage and pleaded for his peers and colleagues to embrace a weave of information.

Wegener wrote:

> Scientists still do not appear to understand sufficiently that all earth sciences must contribute evidence toward unveiling the state of our planet in earlier times, and that the truth of the matter can only be reached by combing all this evidence . . . It is only by combing the information furnished by all the earth sciences that we can hope to determine "truth" here, that is to say, to find the picture that sets out all the known facts in the best arrangement and that therefore has the highest degree of probability. Further, we have to be prepared always for the possibility that each new discovery, no matter what science furnishes it, may modify the conclusions we draw.

When the book was expanded and translated into English in the early 1920s, scientists lined up to dismiss Wegener's findings. In my basic geology text, *Earth*, Wegener appears in a black-and-white photo, taken during a 1912–1913 Greenland expedition (where he traversed 1,200 kilometers of the ice), smoking an enormous German pipe that reaches down from his mouth to his desktop. On the wall to his right, next to a window almost entirely free of frost, two more pipes, one ivory, both longer than the one he smokes. Wegener holds a fountain pen. Photos pinned to the wall include two older people, perhaps parents, five pastoral scenes, presumably Germany. In his time, Wegener was the subject of persistent scientific ridicule; he died in Greenland in November 1930 while returning from field research at an experimental station called Eismitte.

Bryan Storey's own geologic detective work delved into why supercontinents disintegrate in the first place, why and how they disperse to form smaller continental plates, and his findings on the subject were widely hailed and published in influential journals, including *Nature*.

In a documentary film about fieldwork in the Falklands, Bryan drove a Land Rover across a barren, windswept stretch of rocky road as Nancy Sinatra sang "These Boots Were Made for Walking." Geologists love Antarctica because the vegetation-free terrain offers spectacular views of our lithosphere, Earth's upper, rigid rock layer. Of course, more than 97 percent of it has some degree of ice coverage; which means climbing, roped, across crevasse-threaded fields, often for three or four months at a time. Bryan had done this cumulatively for two and a half years of his twenty years at the esteemed British Antarctic Survey; then he packed up his family to become director of a new, international research center, Gateway Antarctica.

Bryan often shared tales of fieldwork while explaining the history of Antarctic geology. One afternoon, Bryan said, "You can have plans, ideas, and dreams. You can have all the gear and financial backing necessary. But in the end, the Antarctic decides what, exactly, you get to do there."

He then recounted a time their camp was knocked into the sea by storm-driven waves. Stranded on a beach, their scheduled pickup ship delayed by fierce weather, Bryan and his survival expert had to revert to Plan B, or surviving Antarctica when your food and gear disappears. They radioed the pickup ship and were told it could be three days or three weeks or three months. All their food, clothing, and rock specimens arduously collected over months had been staged at the shoreline, awaiting the ship that would take them home.

Checking what was left, they found a tent, some fuel, a stove, and sleeping bags. All they needed was food. So they looked around; fishing was not an option. The only other shore occupants were penguins, gentoos and chinstraps. They decided to kill what they would need for a few days' meals. So this was the scene, months away from family, gathering physical evidence to support a nagging notion of how the world came together and then split apart, only to be thwarted by a wave.

When Bryan told this story, he pulled his beard. "I didn't like going after the penguins, they do nothing to get away, really," he said. He had killed chickens on the family farm in Ireland, could penguins be too different? In short, he found the answer was yes.

"With a chicken you can pull it, and twist it, and snap its neck quickly. Penguin necks stretch like rubber. You pull and turn and they snap back and seem no worse for the exercise!"

To finish the job off, his field assistant introduced a weapon, smacked the penguins in the head, then skinned and cooked them. "They tasted not unlike chicken, I hate to say. Albeit chicken that has been fed a rather oily, fishy diet," Bryan added.

Bryan, ever the scientist, saved the penguin skins, sending them out to be properly preserved on his return to Cambridge. The penguins then found their way to his parents' farm in Ireland, where they sat gathering dust on a piano. I imagined his Irish mum, when asked about the stuffed penguins replying, *yes my son Bryan is with the British Antarctic Survey. No, he doesn't study them; he ate that lot.*

We often sat at a round table in his office, beneath a bulletin board pinned with Antarctic Christmas cards, maps, calendars, and field-camp photos. "There we are," he said, gesturing to a huddle of people in bright parkas seated by a yellow tepee-style tent, "drinking a cup of tea in the Antarctic."

On the wall next to Bryan's desk was one of famed photographer Frank Hurley's shots of *Endurance* gripped in the pack ice, soon to be squeezed to splinters. Bryan redirected my gaze to a map divided into four quadrants. "What you need to keep in mind is this essential time line," he said, pointing to a pastel-colored map on the table. The map depicted land as a large, colorful stain, seeping edges, that in four frames and 100 million years tells the story of all land on the planet.

"In order to see how plate tectonics operated you must," he began, "first ask yourself this: Why did the Gondwanaland continent break apart?" Bryan had spent most of his adult life pondering this question. (The word *tectonics*, I had learned, comes from the Greek *tekton*, to build.)

The question of why Gondwanaland began to come apart, while a simple one, does not seem to invite a single answer, he said. "The story begins 183 million years ago in Early Jurassic times. This was a monstrous volcanic event," he added tapping Gondwanaland with a black pen.

"A seaway formed between West (South America and Africa)

and East Gondwanaland (Antarctica, Australia, India, and New Zealand), with sea-floor spreading in the Somali, Mozambique and possibly Weddell Sea basins. These hot spots led to a progressive separation of the continent into east and west, until 50 million years later, about 130 million years ago, the South Atlantic started to form, and India started to separate."

Geologists continue to offer varying theories on why the sea floor spread apart. Bryan drew a diagram showing a cross-section of two continents, with a spreading depression between them. "Constructive plate boundaries," he said. "Into this space, basalt flowed, moved perhaps by convection currents. Think of this movement like a duvet falling from your bed. A third of it slips down to the floor then the rest follows, moving with its own weight. We believe it's the same thing with the spreading sea floor."

"At 100 million years ago, New Zealand and Australia began to split from the Antarctic core, and other small continental blocks—Madagascar and the Seychelles—separated from India as it migrated northwards away from Africa and Antarctica. Things began to speed up.

"At 85 million years, New Zealand waved good-bye to Antarctica," he said. "The last bit to break off from Antarctica was the Drake Passage—the notorious channel of rough seas separating the Antarctic Peninsula from South America—this last bit was particularly important because it led to the development of the circumpolar current. The first ice appeared at 35 million years, although there was no permanent ice until a mere 20 million years ago. Since then, it has advanced and retreated," he continued.

I sat down with a stack of geology books, found this written in an encyclopedia, under "continental drift,"

> The theory of continental drift was not generally accepted, particularly by American geologists, until the 1950s and 60s, when

a group of British geophysicists reported on magnetic studies of rocks from many places and from each major division of geologic time. They found that for each continent, the magnetic pole had apparently changed position through geologic time, forming a smooth curve, or pole path, particular to that continent. The pole paths for Europe and North America could be made to coincide by bringing the continents together.

When Harry Hess, a mid-twentieth century Princeton geologist, presented his own work on the topic, advancing important ideas about the sea floor spreading, he subtitled his paper "an essay in geopoetry."

Seven

Only by the merest happenstance did he escape the private logic of that ice world.

—Thomas Pynchon, V

All expeditions begin as idea and then become list—a series of related words arranged in an order—and Antarcticans deploy their lists as structure, guideline, lifeline. Each story I found and read and considered became a square of orange paper on a corkboard, resembling Tibetan prayer flags in their final string. Details, moments, symbols, ready to be examined for clues, like a woman walking to the South Pole scans the horizon. Like Wegener's plea that we embrace new ideas, no matter what discipline offers them to us. Can artists make sense of exploration in factually relevant ways? Don't we experience the world of blue-sky geographic ambition each time we sit down with the wide, white page?

We could only go ashore in Antarctica with one of the specially trained survival experts. When we clambered down the ship's side, from swinging rope ladder to bobbing rubber boat, these experts would remind us of this: Check your packs one more time. If you forget something in Antarctica, you die. At first, this commentary frightened me. The forgetful were among the dead ones, was the suggestion, should things go wrong. When they would talk about dying, it happened against a backdrop of beautiful place, green/silver/pale melon. Maybe not such a bad place to die.

I think of Antarctica every day. Antarctic stories, those told by the explorers, and basalt and cormorants and penguins and mighty blue ice and all the wild features of that place, a braided whole. For thousands of years the Antarctic has served as our imagined territory. The Antarctic reminds us that infinity may be concept but not fact. Facts: Collapsing, calving, melting before our eyes.

My first look at Antarctica: ice of the Ross Sea, one of the two great Antarctic seas, deep tears into a continent inclined toward a circular shape. I remember standing on the edge of an Adélie penguin rookery, staring at a gray, weathered hut built by Ernest Shackleton eighty years earlier. It reminded me of the house tumbling from the sky in The Wizard of Oz.

What I touched that day was merely old weathered wood, wood in late stages of decay. Was it also the honor, the valor, the dream of those first people to enter a last, unknown world? A little more than ten years after he built the hut and walked to within ninety miles of being first man to the South Pole, Shackleton's heart would fail; he would die among his Antarctic mates on a ship named Quest.

Living in the Antarctic, ice, land, and seas, for months gave me a frame for understanding a landscape difficult to imagine—a grossly magnified view of some strange animal's bone marrow comes to mind, a web, a design, a place where no trees obscure a sort of crazed yet inviting linearity. It is a place, like Yosemite or Lyttelton or the red cliffs of Zion, whose outlines you can feel like a finger running down your spine.

The stories were best when they spoke to what I felt in Antarctica; people placed themselves into its skeletal landscape and then came stories, like the sound of tambourines.

What is a *polar junkie?* My friend the great historian Baden Norris has told the stories of Antarctic exploration for forty years. He is a polar explorer—he has been there a dozen times. I know polar junkies well: All Antarctica, all the time. Grim news bits like the drowning of a British marine biologist by a leopard seal, Russians drilling into never-touched Lake Vostok, glacial ice moving with the cycle of the moon, a seal-tooth bracelet for sale at auction, then, who sold it, who bought it, and for how much? Polar junkies love rosters, line-ups, who's-who style recountings of expeditions. Names and birthplaces of bygone explorers, what they did in World Wars, where they are buried, whether their descendants are polar junkies, too.

The ordinariness of Antarctic sailors' temperate lives suggests maybe you could be like them too, if you had the chance. You could go to sea, live on the ice, eat penguins, you could be good spirited and show what you were made of. Most people don't get a chance to show what they are made of.

People assume if you like Antarctica, you like cold. There is little documentary evidence to support this; however, most Antarcticans do have a fondness for ice. Antarctic ice makes a lively addition to a cocktail. Melting in alcohol, accelerated, pings, old air set free.

When I first told my father I was going to Antarctica, he reminded me of my childhood fixation on the *Titanic.* He recalled watching a black-and-white film of the sinking at a summer drive-in, and how I had nightmares for months.

Months, he reminded me. "And you were maybe five years old. All you talked about was icebergs!"

Penguin guano, or excrement, brings to mind Union Carbide atrocities. The instructions given after visiting a rookery were simple: Strip on the ship's deck. Do not let even a speck of that guano inside the ship.

Penguins and their stink make an impression. Once you smell them in the wild, you can never watch animated or actual footage film, gaze at a postcard, or hold a glass penguin chess piece and not recall that sense memory. Stuffed penguins decorating toy stores at Christmas: I smell guano. At the Canterbury Museum they reassembled Cape Hallett as an exhibit, a performance of the mundane, enlivened by where the buildings had once been, like looking at one of the Apollo capsules. Real, actual old wood that used to be in Antarctica, lived in by real, actual men with beards. I smelled it before I saw it. Penguins had inhabited the lower recesses of the buildings. I saw people in the museum look down and check their shoes, had someone stepped in something? No, this is penguin guano, thousands of miles from home. One of the curators told me the smell was particularly hard on the school children who came to hear of Cape Hallett, because they were forced to sit on the floor by the exhibit: The closer you get to the base of the structures, she said, the more disgusting the smell is.

While penguin faces remain fixed in the same placid expression, the manner they hold their flippers, or pad over sea-smoothed, gray, volcanic rocks on thick orange feet, communicates a feeling both determined and at peace with their cold choices. Penguins choose freedom from predation over weather.

They find something divine in towering ice, floes white against a navy blue sea.

Penguins are the representative Antarctican figure appearing on wind chimes, long underwear, hats, coffee mugs, stuffed toys sporting bright bows, stationery, car decals, stained-glass doors, tea towels, underpants, ashtrays, backpacks, life-size inflated versions standing three feet tall. Penguins, tough survivors, birds who conjure ocean as sky. Like all Antarcticans, they like to disappear, beneath waves, behind ice; like all Antarcticans they believe ice is nice. I have never seen penguin décor recorded in a book. The living memory of penguins at sea against the representation of them is so shocking to me. Do we embrace them because of their superficial lure—even black and white, a clumsy demeanor that says, cute? I think we follow them because of their evasion of the temperate, their blue-and green-colored world, their unreachable lives, their orgiastic existence in Antarctica.

According to Baden, the penguins became a standard feature of homes in Lyttelton during the early days of the twentieth century. Badly stuffed, unnaturally posed, they stood in the vestibule ready for all guests, just as they do on the rocky beaches of Antarctica. If you go there, you will see them placidly standing on gray, rocky beaches, waiting with a certainty that says, we have been expecting you. If you are still among them, they will stand very close to you, touch you with their beaks. Penguins rarely run from the new, although I have read that the sound of helicopters disrupts their sex lives. I imagine this could be said to be something we have in common with penguins. Hollywood could have told the scientists this fact, that helicopters freak us all out; when directors want a sense urgency, they throw in a helicopter whizzing onto the scene, men with shiny helmets and reflective glasses. It disrupts my sex life just thinking about it.

"Everyone has an Antarctic," says Hugh Godolphin on page 241 of Thomas Pynchon's novel V. In Antarctican circles, this line is widely quoted. There are ten more references in V that can be construed as Antarctic in nature, yet none of these has caught on in the same way, including, "What sends the English into these terrible places?" (p. 204); "I have been at the Pole" (p. 205); "the cold tongue of a current from the Antarctic south" (p. 266); "cold as Antarctica" (p. 271); or my favorite, "Only by the merest happenstance did he escape the private logic of that ice world" (p. 484).

We all dream of it—the landscape rises like a vapor, whirls around in the clouds, goes looking for receptive minds. It seeped into Frank Worsley's head one night as he slumbered. He dreamt of walking down Burlington Street in London navigating a street filled with ice blocks. He noted what a curious dream it was, yet felt strangely compelled to retrace the path, so in the morning he wandered down Burlington Street, looked up, saw a sign, *Imperial Trans-Antarctic Expedition*, climbed the stairs, presented himself to Shackleton and Frank Wild, and told them how he had been lured to their doorstep by a dream. Seamen are superstitious. Wild and Shackleton saw this able man as sent to them by an act of grace. It was his fate. Little did they know this act of grace would be of the most extraordinary kind: Here was the man who would save their lives. *Here was their savior.*

In Christchurch's Anglican cathedral, built on the central square, a mass blesses and returns the Chalice of the Snows, a silver goblet that travels between the cathedral of stone and the cathedral of ice that is Antarctica. James Clark Ross first brought the chalice south on his ships *Terror* and *Erebus* in the mid-nineteenth century.

   Spring and summer in Antarctica, fall and winter in New Zealand. Two Antarctic plaques decorate the church; one memorialized those who died in Antarctica, the other offered thanks for a gift from the U.S. government to New Zealand for supporting American Antarctic explorations during much of the twentieth century.

Christchurch remains the Ross Sea region's gateway city—polar-bound ships continue to sail from Lyttelton, more than 150 flights wing south each summer season, stuffed with thousands of scientists, survival experts, other Antarcticans all trussed like turkeys in cold-weather gear.

The Christchurch economy and social scene expand and heave under the flow heading to and from Antarctica. They fill hotels and pubs awaiting a lift on a C-130 cargo plane. Strolling down Worcester Boulevard, traversed by restored historic trams, lined with lipstick-red telephone booths like those once ubiquitous in London, you pass the new Robert McDougall Art Gallery, where the Tait Room is devoted solely to work created by artists who travel to Antarctica for inspiration. Baden and I attended the inaugural show in the Tait Room, where polar diatoms—siliceous micro-organisms, one-celled alga whose shells then form diatomaceous ooze on the ocean's bottom—were recreated in wood.

Three to five feet in length, these replicas were suspended from the ceiling, painted with fluorescent pigments, and lit with black light. They looked like cartoonish African tribal shields. Monitors showed diatoms squidging along in their natural environment. As we left the gallery, Baden and I exchanged raised-eyebrow glances.

A block away, across the Avon River, Robert Falcon Scott kept watch, carved in Carrara marble by his widow, Kathleen. She then donated the statue to the city that offered her husband money and acclaim in his lifetime. Its twin stands in London.

Follow the river to the Town Hall, scene of the annual U.S. National Science Foundation Polar Program dinner, kicking off the summer research season in Antarctica. I attended the dinner as a guest of Lou Sanson, CEO of New Zealand's huge Antarctic stake, the Ross Dependency. New Zealand was bequeathed the Ross territory by Great Britain in the 1930s, and manages all logistics there; Antarctica New Zealand is a government subsidiary, run as a land management business whose main focus is supporting scientific research.

It was a cold September night, winds blasting up from the south: Antarctica calling. I stood in the reception line with Lou, an affable, outdoorsy Kiwi, and Leslie McTurk, an imposing woman dressed in a Chanel-style suit, with heavily sprayed and dyed blonde hair. Lou had invited her down to Antarctica to have a look around; she was a city council member and he ran a continuous shuttle of New Zealand politicos to Antarctica. Good for business, I imagined. Travel to Antarctica under government programs requires extensive medical evaluations, including a mandatory syphilis test. McTurk amused the line by recounting her own day at the hospital: "Everyone at the hospital knew who I was, and there I stood, asking for the syphilis screening. Then I said I needed it for Antarctica. I don't think anyone believed me." We edged forward in the line, three deep and a hundred people long, to the smiling U.S. ambassador, a banker and Republican fundraiser named Butch Swindells. To the right of the ambassador, National Science Foundation officials and American military aviators, wearing shiny gold, red, and green decorations.

The Antarctic Heritage Trail, a brochure, offers an illustration of Antarctica and New Zealand against a pale blue sea, latitude and longitude lines giving it a sense of order and time. New Zealand appears tethered by long red dashes to a labeled blue-dot South Pole, as though New Zealand might float away across the grid without Antarctica, or vice versa. New Zealand is colored bright green, Antarctica, white.

Lyttelton occupies stops four and five on the eight-stop trail. The brochure shows the main display in the Antarctic gallery, four mannequins dressed in donated Antarctic field clothes. The brochure tells us the Antarctic gallery relays (interesting choice of words) the history of Lyttelton's association with Antarctic exploration. Point 5 on the trail is the Lyttelton Harbour and Wharf. The sepia-toned photograph shows Shackleton's ship Nimrod surrounded by throngs of women in long white dresses and men in hats.

The departure of Nimrod was the highlight of Lyttelton's annual regatta in 1908. The fifty-thousand-strong crowd, Baden Norris estimates, was the largest number of people to ever gather in Lyttelton. Shackleton's book, The Heart of the Antarctic, captures the moment, "such a farewell and God-speed from New Zealand as left no man of us unmoved."

Reading Antarcticans' letters and other personal papers from those early days, talking with today's polar explorers, there is a unifying undercurrent to their stories—what you could call a pleasing crudeness to Antarctic endeavors. When ships were stuck in ice, the crew got out and dynamited the ice. If they had no dynamite, they used picks. Long passages of seamens' journals are devoted to this activity. Scott almost lost Discovery to the ice, and James Paton's diary in the Canterbury Museum talks about off-loading all the ship's supplies and the endless digging of ice. I reckon it was a good thing those men had not an aerial view of what they were up against. Could you imagine that? I can hear them now: "I'm not digging that fucking ice." For entertainment, they staged drag shows. They erected a polar theater using canvas from the ship as a curtain and acted out farces and romantic comedies. They printed newspapers and wrote poetry and painted watercolors of the sunsets. It all seems rather folksy, in their rustic bunkhouse, lined with men in thick sweaters, smoking pipes. Like an extreme summer camp for people with the polar bug.

You hear it in stories of South Pole workers forming a peace sign with their bodies on the ice, and in tales of traversing glaciers, told by tough scientists as tears well in their eyes. *We did not think we were going to make it.* So. This is beginning and leitmotif. Always the idea that Antarctica triumphs, plays its steady game of cold, wind, crevasse. Always the idea it will be there for us, guarded by fierce seas, shrouded in cold, hard ice.

Eight

In the world of words, the imagination is one of the forces of nature.

—Wallace Stevens

On what often passed for a summer's day in Christchurch, wind ripping up from the south, Antarctic-cold, rattling windows and sending tree branches flying, I sat sipping coffee at my Gateway Antarctica office, a stream of commentary running between me and Michelle Finnemore, an American in her thirties whose office was directly across the hall. If I asked nicely, Finnemore told me funny stories about living at the South Pole, although with the caveat I could not put them into my book. Finnemore came from a large Catholic family in Pittsburgh, made an hour-long bike ride to work many days, and took yoga classes at lunch. She was a compact and fit person and often referenced weekends spent riding across trails, sinews of rock shards cut in great brown, barren stretches of the Canterbury Plain. She claimed to have liked living at the South Pole, under the metal dome, and when I would press her for details of capsular living, life under a dome in a hostile physical landscape clearly a point of fixation for most cultures, see Jules Verne or Stanislaus Lem for instance, encouraged me to "make up whatever you want."

When I went to her home once for an evening of food and wine, she had deliberately arranged penguin-themed hand towels for my benefit, based on a comment I made that Antarcticans often had penguins represented in their homes, which in turn had been a reference to a recent spate of interviews with Antarcticans at home, during which I discovered Bryan had custom-made stained-glass doors depicting emperor penguins, while other Antarcticans displayed smaller glass versions on low, dark-wood coffee tables, penguins made in the famed glass-blowing operation in the New Zealand town of Hokitika. (You could even buy a glass penguin chess set.)

She thought this to be a sort of white-wash of Antarcticans, a calling out of details that defined norms of the subculture that then existed only because I had chosen to push them to the surface; she also seemed to hold the unshakeable belief that the sort of writing I set out to accomplish was based on my own interest in marginal stories about the personal lives of Antarcticans, a *People*-magazine lens on a continent, stories that did hold me ever-so-slightly in their thrall but were no different than stories from any other continent and in this failed the test I had established for all of this research, earlier mentioned here: If this had happened some place other than Antarctica would it be noted or is it noted because it happened here? Man falls off hut here. Film at 11. With penguins. (Among the stories I could not, would not tell, of course, were tales of an Antarctica New Zealand board member so drunk on the ice she had to be carried from the bar to a plane, simmering speculation that Shackleton was bisexual, and a local historian who liked to stand naked atop tabular icebergs.) I had once tried to argue with her that I thought Antarctica held the title of highest rate of sex per capita.

Finnemore studied and taught the Antarctic Treaty as a

legal and political document and brought the experience of life at the South Pole to its discussion in the classroom. She had logged fourteen months in total at the South Pole, in a place named Amundsen-Scott by Admiral Richard E. Byrd. The average monthly temperatures range from −18 degrees Fahrenheit in January to −76 degrees in July. The polar ice—a slow, frozen tide edging toward the coast—moves about thirty feet a year. South Pole inhabitants, Polies, are reported to be either the most solid or the most insane people on the planet.

Finnemore and I, during our morning cross-hall shout-chats, a habit that undoubtedly unglued our European colleagues at Gateway, calling out in loud voices and gum chewing being two definitional and alarming American characteristics, discussed the expanded South Pole station the United States began building in 2000; the estimated time to completion had been seven years, given the very brief window of work time at the South Pole. When it was finished, her former home (an aluminum geodesic dome, 165 feet in diameter at its base and 55 feet at its apex—surviving the Pole necessitated complete isolation from the weather) was dismantled and removed, thus vanishing from historical view. I imagined the old dome like a large aluminum bowl plunked down on a tiny town.

When I asked how she felt about the dome, Finnemore said, "It kept me alive. I loved that dome."

She wondered why they couldn't make it into a museum in a more northerly clime. Wouldn't people want to see a real South Pole station?

This sounded a bit peculiar to me and I called across the hall, "Where would it live? In the Arizona desert like the London Bridge?" Would the dome make sense to people if there wasn't Antarctica stretching for miles in all directions, ready to turn all who left its comfort into a frozen slab of meat?

And yet, as we spoke, a base called Hallett, which had been built at Cape Hallett in the Ross Sea, and which I had visited when it was perhaps the most godforsaken wreck of a place, having been abandoned by the U.S. and New Zealand governments, was displayed at the Canterbury Museum, resurrected as a museum display. (The days with Greenpeace at Cape Hallett remain clear in my recollection. Late February 1988 and the wind came ripping across the ice. Adélie penguins lived at Cape Hallett—having been pushed aside when the base was constructed in the 1950s and then slowly reclaiming it as the people abandoned the place. Like squatters, the Adélies hopped on their flubbery feet amid fuel barrels rusted and frozen and ready to spring a leak. The acrid smell of penguin guano filled the air. I left. I stood on the ship's bridge with binoculars and stared at Greenpeace people, Maggie, Bernadette, Bob, working to get the fuel out of the old barrels into new barrels. Many years later, when I gave a talk about this unwitnessed bravery, a New Zealand government official said, "We were going to clean up Hallett anyway. Greenpeace had no effect on us." I doubted him as he said this, for I recalled when Greenpeace first took photos of the Antarctic mess made by scientific research stations. There were many ways to deny Greenpeace a place in Antarctic histories, but saying they didn't hurry or prompt actual tidying cut no ice with me. First they took the photos, then the photos were in newspapers around the world, then the clean-up began. It was pure populist activism at its best. I smiled at the man who denied their agency. Wanker. Yes, times don't change regarding the privileging of stories. First you cut out the illiterate sailors, later you erase dozens of people asking for environmental justice.)

Antarctic stories have always migrated north in a capricious manner. When the earliest polar explorers, Shackleton and Scott, donated their used gear to the Canterbury Museum

between 1901 and 1912, it was piled into a basement corner, there to stay until the 1970s. The balaclavas, skis, lamps,
anoraks, goggles didn't animate any story deemed interesting to the public; the gear, used, broken, tangled, equipment failing in its task to bring back all men alive, would
be resurrected six decades later, when three museums in
the greater Christchurch area lured eager viewers with that
same gear as the twenty-first century opened. Taste and perspective change.

Finnemore's imagined display of the uber-dome: I closed
my eyes and tried to pull together all the fragments of information I had about South Pole life, twenty-seven people living under a dome, buried under snow, far from the known
world. I tried not to picture them upside down, hanging off
the bottom of the world.

My careful imaginings came to an abrupt end when the
phone rang; it was an assistant producer calling from Auckland, the North Island city considered New Zealand's big
smoke, home to the media, hot weather, and a vibrant Polynesian culture almost entirely absent from waspy Christchurch.
The woman asked me if I would be interested in appearing on
The Breakfast Programme, the New Zealand equivalent to The
Today Show. They had read about my research and wanted me
to talk about the "little known" stories of Antarctic exploration. The main host, a man named Mike Hosking, possessed
a Gatling-gun style of interviewing, which I enjoyed watching in the morning before taking my children to school. He
made snarky comments about the guests. I said yes without
too much thought.

Meanwhile, Antarcticans seemed to tumble from the sky in
New Zealand. It is hard for me to quantify, although I was
told that everyone had either been to Antarctica or someone
in their extended family had been there. Here's how days

would unfurl, the taxi driver taking me to Lyttelton telling me stories about working as a carpenter at McMurdo, in a riverside café the waitress offers she recently applied to go south, a man at the bus stop sees my penguin key chain and says he used to study them at Cape Royds in the Ross Sea. It felt like home. I tried not to contrast this with my colleagues in America, some of whom did not know if the Antarctic was the North or the South Pole. Most had no idea what lived there, and the preferred comment was, why go there?

Lou Sanson, who managed New Zealand's Ross Dependency, explained that in New Zealand everyone had either been to Antarctica, was trying to go, or was related to someone who had. Lou's own father, he explained, had been stationed at Scott Base in the 1960s. There is no equivalent geographic phenomenon in the United States that comes to mind.

Two weeks later, high winds blasting across the Tasman Sea tossed our Auckland-bound plane around the sky. I was en route to my television debut. I had missed my scheduled flight, lost in conversation with Keith Springer, an experienced polar survival expert who managed New Zealand's Scott Base. We swapped stories of life on Ross Island, walking around Cape Evans and its ghostly historic hut. He had been at McMurdo when the Greenpeace ship I was on came in; Keith recalled the rather menacing threats made to New Zealand contract workers. Talk to Greenpeace and you are on the first plane home. My fellow passengers calmly peered out the windows while our 737 rolled side to side like a doomed rock-and-roll star's Cessna. I sat in seat 11B, white knuckled, staring straight ahead, trying not to scream.

It poured rain from a sun-filled sky as we landed, then a perfect rainbow appeared, offering a shade of lavender almost sublime. Hard to stay rattled with that sky as theater.

In the evening I walked around downtown Auckland, a

cement-bound landscape spreading out under the watchful eye of the Sky Tower, an architectural concept I despise. It loomed over us, comfortable in its blue-lit concrete splendor; people laughed and ate meals in glowing, glass-sided restaurants stacked in the mall at its base. In a tiny sushi bar, picking through a bento box of creatively sculpted carrot flowers and salmon sashimi, wondering why appearing on live television ever sounded like an interesting idea. When I returned to the hotel, I climbed fifteen floors to the rooftop pool deck and stood alone at the glass rail, looking out over a deep violet Auckland harbor ringed in pale cinnamon lights. So alive with yachts and cafés, the same quayside where French divers attacked the Greenpeace ship *Rainbow Warrior* and blew her up. The man they killed was just a photographer trying to record the story, just a father interested in making the world OK for his children. I turned and looked the other way, up at the hotel tower, and saw a couple slowly undressing each other, a tiny stage illuminated in the night. I walked back toward the elevators. Good for them, I thought. Good for them.

At 8:15 a.m. the next morning, a Maori security guard ushered me into the green room, talking soothingly all the while about the weather. The green room was actually deep taupe, filled with posters by Klee, Picasso, and Klimt. A large TV in the corner blasted out the morning show and its snappy non-music DA-da-da-da-DA-DA. A fashion designer was on the screen, in a white, fluffy blouse, talking about her new line. She laughed and said witty things about hemlines. This television appearance was not a good call on my part.

I heard the host approaching during a commercial break—funny how television voices hang in your head in a peculiar way; he talked and whistled.

Mike Hosking stood about five foot five and wore what

looked like a painfully tight suit: navy blue with a thin white stripe, five buttons fastened the jacket into place. It reminded me of the '70s cult show The Prisoner; I imagined the bouncing white ball coming our way. A woman beckoned me into a cramped make-up room filled with hot white light.

The room was loud with chatter as hairstylists and make-up artists buzzed around. "Did you see what she wore? Who books these people," someone yelped.

I was shown a seat and the make-up woman talked of doing makeup for Lord of the Rings. I wondered if her time had been spent with orcs, or elves, or dwarves. She sponged a tan color all over my face, the way you might roll primer on bare walls—television washes you out, she said, and then made my mouth bright cranberry.

"What about your hair?" she asked. Her own hair was black, shingled, short, and featured a pale lavender stripe.

"Well," I said, "this is how I wear it." She lifted a hank in the back and let it fall, then sighed. "How about I put some gloss in it?"

I balanced my new face on the green room couch. A gang of women and men, in their mid-twenties, toting instruments and mike stands, wandered in; one announced they were Barrage, a Canadian performance group doing a four-night gig at the Auckland Arts festival. The newspaper had called them the new Riverdance, which struck me as an unfortunate comparison. One asked what my gig was. Before I could answer, the documentary filmmaker in their entourage broke into a loud, wailing story about their harrowing fifty-hour flight from Canada: Vancouver–Los Angeles–Taipei–Singapore–Auckland.

And then I was led away to the set.

Mike settled in on his couch—incredibly tight suit tight like a tourniquet around his waist—and glanced at questions on the table. The first line in all caps WHAT IS AN ANTARCTICAN?

When the break ended, Mike interviewed me like I was in trouble for something. A tone of, so you're a writer who's come here *looking for stories?*

Hasn't everything been said about Antarctica in the many books already published? What are these new or unknown stories? How do people live there? What is the class system? Wasn't it an environment under threat? Weren't they building hotels there?

In these situations, you are meant to do something called a "pivot"—redirecting the interviewer by answering the question however you desire. So I asked Hosking if he had been to Antarctica.

No, no, he laughed.

I suggested he should call Shelly, who handled the media for Antarctica New Zealand, and get on a press junket south. "You could do the show down there, and take Kate along with you."

He looked at the camera and said he preferred to spend his vacations in Fiji. But I was doing a good promotion job. They cut to Kate the blond newsreader at the news desk, laughing. Surely four minutes had passed. I deployed Thoreau— paraphrasing, we all need to know there is one place completely wild and free, without which we will surely go insane. Antarctica, I concluded, was that place. We all better mind it didn't melt or become overrun with scientists.

Hosking looked surprised by Thoreau. He segued, talking to the camera about Dido's new album as her haunting soprano played in the background.

It was a gray day in Auckland as I ran back to the hotel. In the lobby, I ordered a coffee and skulked off to check my email. The Canterbury Antarcticans flashed in via the screen. Professor Bryan Storey sent a message from Gateway with the subject line "Our Star!" Then lauded me for not saying anything controversial.

A nor'west wind kicked up leaves as I walked around Auckland, outer-space Sky Tower as my signpost. I thought about an object in the Canterbury Polar Gallery, a long, knitting-needle-like tool. It had been used to pierce emperor penguin eggs one bitter, cold June in Antarctic darkness, a quest that inspired one of the most moving, dramatic, and evocative of all Antarctican stories: *The Worst Journey in the World*. Apsley Cherry-Garrard wrote of exploring on Ross Island, and includes a scene where he anticipates the arrival of a curator to take the penguin eggs for further study. His mind wanders, recalling his two companions, Wilson and a tough man named Bowers, a ferocious Antarctic winter landscape, encased in night, utter cold, and a jumble of ice. He waits a long time for someone to accept what he has brought from the bottom of the world, enormous eggs from the largest living penguins on the planet. He waits with ghosts; both his companions dead six months after this egg-hunt expedition, starving and freezing returning from the pole. In London, the museum staff cannot be bothered. Cherry-Garrard witnesses the last step of their perilous explorations, a cold, hard bench, dismissive guards, and in the end, an indifferent home for his delicate treasures.

Field Notes

Loneliness. Fantasy. Desire.

Nine

I don't go for fancy cars
For diamond rings
Or movie stars
I go for penguins
—Lyle Lovett, "Penguins" (1994)

Prior to sailing to Antarctica, the bulk of my penguin contact came via cartoons: Chilly Willy and Tennessee Tuxedo and Opus. I've never been one for wildlife books or calendars, nor even for *National Geographic* or "wilderness" specials, preferring to either be outside—or not.

The first penguins I encountered were Adélies, *Pygoscelis adeliae*—named by the French polar explorer Dumont D'Urville in honor of his wife. They swam along beside the ship as we cruised into the Ross Sea. Penguins at sea do a Clark Kent–to–Superman transformation. They glide, speed, and generally command attention. What struck me was how they bore little resemblance to their onshore bumbling selves— shiny, glossed leather footballs in the water, hurtling along. I watched them through binoculars and wondered about their lives. They seemed to have required an unusually rigorous series of adaptations.

Penguins spend well over half, and some as much as three-quarters, of their lives at sea. Emperor penguins, *Aptenodytes forsteri,* swim an estimated six to seven miles an hour but have been clocked at an ecstatic nine miles an hour. The emperor is the largest of seventeen penguin species, averaging forty-five inches in length and weighing up to eighty-eight pounds, and chooses to live in isolated Antarctic colonies and nowhere else in the world. In the winter they live on the Antarctic continent.

Seeing this act, flying-in-water bird, gives more than a momentary pause. Seeing this act, a stereoscope of bird, water, sky, air, light, I grasped why penguins have been anchored in our imaginations and histories since first recorded in the fifteenth century.

The first penguin fossils were found in New Zealand during the mid-nineteenth century; thirty-two extinct penguin species have been recorded to date. The *Palaeudyptes antarcticus* lived during the Eocene Period, 38 to 42 million years ago, and stood about five feet tall. In the Miocene Period, 11 to 25 million years ago, *Pachydyptes ponderosus* ambled along the New Zealand coast. Scientists estimate it may have weighed as much as three hundred pounds. It would be a more interesting world if *Pachydyptes ponderosus* remained among us; imagine one of those penguins emerging from the sea. Why did the human-sized penguins vanish? Researchers reason the supersized penguins disappeared as smaller whales and prehistoric seals appeared on the scene, either because they couldn't compete successfully for food or because they became dinner.

When I first encountered penguins on land, at the huge Adélie penguin encampment at Cape Royds, home to a historic Shackleton hut, they could not have been more engaging. Adélies sport crisp, white bellies and ebony backs, wings, and heads. I simply squatted on my heels on the perimeter of their colony, and bold individuals wandered over to me. One touched me with its beak. Then, satisfied with their examination, three stood next to me, gazing out at the silver sea. We stayed this way for some time. Later, I asked our resident animal biologist what it was all about. "They were most likely wondering what sort of penguin you were," she said.

I decided to read in detail about penguins. One story has the word *penguin* evolving from the Welsh *pen gwyn*, meaning "white head." It was originally the name of the now-extinct great auk of the North Atlantic; great auks also could not fly and were also killed off easily by sailors, who ate them. The word was reportedly pronounced "pin wing" in Newfoundland, however, and some believe the name is a description of the auk's more flipperlike thin wings. As early as 1588 the southern bird we know as penguin shows up in references. Some scholars believe the birds' stubby stature influenced their name, coming from the Latin word *pinguis*, meaning "stout" or "fat."

Penguins are Southern Hemisphere–only inhabitants and can also be found in New Zealand, South Australia, and off the Peruvian, Chilean, and South African coasts. The Galapagos Islands are their farthest point north. Here the world's only willingly tropical penguins fish and bask.

The architecture of penguins' glistening black, white, and gray feather coats amazes: on some, seventy feathers per square inch. In their unobstructed landscape, hopping from cold sea to ice often means facing a howling wind. Penguins are beautifully engineered to meet the demands of Antarctica. Their delicate feathers wick water away. *Adaptation.*

Perhaps penguins have found the cold is worth it. They'd rather tough out that world than try to make sense of our warmer version. In the winter, emperors survive temperatures that dip to −50 degrees Celsius.

Whatever their rationale, they certainly are not telling.

While emperor penguins may be the bread-and-butter of glossy wildlife calendars, standing tall and barrel-chested, they are not imbued with expressive faces. Or not expressive in a manner that codes well for human consumption. Like all their bird kin, they have been blessed with physiognomies that hide what is in their hearts.

Emperor penguins dazzle: They can dive to depths of nine hundred feet and stay down for minutes at a time. When they mate in winter, a single egg is laid, then the males of the colony form a comma-shaped huddle. The females swim out to sea. The males remain, gathering and shifting against the screaming wind, outer bodies shuffling to the center for warmth. They build no nests, choosing to balance an egg on webbed feet, nestling it in a flap of protective skin. Huddle, shuffle, move. Survival means working together.

One researcher noted that before 1998, there was no environmental impact on Ross Sea emperor populations. Now we can watch what warmer climates globally mean for these die-hard over-winterers.

One night I sat in a University of Canterbury lecture hall, listening to a scientist discuss why some birds choose not to fly. "It takes a lot of energy to fly," he said, shrugging. He pulled on a ginger beard. "Once birds don't need to, once predators stop forcing them into the air, they don't mind staying on the ground. This is where the penguin seems to have landed."

So. It seemed more like they found solace in their choice, a simple beauty in the fact of their own lives. There are a thousand and one things that pull birds in warmer climes down to Earth. Maybe penguins had a solid, species-wide memory of this list, shared stories from the old days of flight during their long, quiet hours on the floes.

While the Antarctic is well publicized as the coldest place on Earth, extreme cold is hard for we tropically adapted animals to bring to mind. There are the great Inuit peoples of the Arctic who have adapted their lives to the cold. But cold is cold. Inuit histories are marked by starvation and hardship wrought from cold. We are not designed for it. Numbers used to describe cold challenge the imagination.

How do you bring to mind double-digit figures in the negative? All of us are familiar with what we call cold winter winds: wind-chill factor. The Americans Paul Siple and Charlie Passel first developed the old wind chill index in 1939–1941. Their model was based on the amount of time it took a cylinder of water to freeze. But scientists felt they could improve on the pan of water model. So, the Joint Action Group for Temperature Indices was put together in the United States and Canada to reconsider how we describe the cold known as wind chill. In 2001, the U.S. National Weather Service officially introduced a new method of calculating wind chill, which takes into account modern heat transfer theory.

Ten

Superhuman effort isn't worth a damn unless it achieves results.

—Ernest Shackleton

It's just a mildewed book with a cracked spine, pages slipping free, glue long since gone to dust. The book rested on my desk, next to a cascading pile of 1950s era U.S. Navy pictures of Antarctica, many of which show airplanes looking like silver toys on a white sandy beach. *Antarctica* (1960, photography by Emil Schulthess) had caught Michelle Finnemore's discerning eye at a Christchurch garage sale and she bargained it down to 50 cents. Her note said, "Check out the photos of the store."

Antarctica documents Operation High Jump II, and among its black-and-white photos is one of men gathered in an Antarctic shop, circa 1956. The caption reads,

> *Every Antarctic station has its store. On Byrd Station, the store is under the control of Lt. Edward J. Galla, military leader in charge and station doctor. The most popular items are cigarettes, tobacco, beer, toothpaste and soap, although the stock is by no means limited to these and also includes films, flashbulbs, etc.*

Four slick-haired men lined up along a high, wooden counter; one chewed a toothpick amid a wide, white grin. A man, Doctor Galla I presume, wore thick glasses, stood opposite ticking off items in a thick ledger. Signs tacked to the door stated, Beer and Soda, Tues–Thurs 1800–TO–1815 and Hip's Store, Mon–Wed–Fri 1800–TO–1830. Tiny packets of Tide laundry detergent, some upside down, lined a shelf, next to Baby Ruth candy bars; a dozen onyx rosaries dangled from rafters—in case you made it all the way to Antarctica and realized your rosary was back in Wisconsin. The Tide packets carbon date the scene: nothing ages as perfectly and incontrovertibly in the modern age as product packaging. None of the men appeared sun-or windburned; no one was disheveled or sported wild hair. Careful scrutiny of the photos revealed nothing about their clothes or the camp-store scene signaling they were even in the Antarctic: It could be the Poconos.

Antarctic shops had become a fascination of mine after a chance encounter with Robert Isles, former tank driver and current manager of bar and retail sales in the Ross Dependency. I met him during a book launch at the Canterbury Museum, where I lurked in the back with Peter Fuchs, son of the great Antarctic explorer Vivian "Bunny" Fuchs, drinking red wine. The book being launched offered a new round of photos capturing the Scott hut at Cape Evans. Peter and I were bored. The cabernet-merlot blend bore a Scott Base label and showed a picture of Scott's hut at Cape Evans. "How very unusual," Peter noted, holding the gold and claret label closer for a better look. "I better get some to take back to the U.K." The bartender heard us and pointed out a man sporting a silver crewcut. Bob Isles handed me his card, and invited me to visit him at Burnham Military Camp on the outskirts of Christchurch, where he ran the business when not in Antarctica. (Burnham had its own link to Antarctica as the site

Frank Arthur Worsley as he appeared on his Red Cross identification papers at the outset of World War II.

of a first-aid training for the 1957–1958 Trans-Antarctic Expedition.) About a month later, I drove to the camp—it had the vaguely dilapidated, sagging feel that hangs over military housing, rows of white, single-story clapboard buildings, rectangular barracks, brick homes, and a small school with windows covered in faded, blue-tissue snowflakes, all

wrapped in gleaming silver razor wire; soldiers in full camouflage gear marched in neat, rectangular groups.

I needed directions to Bob Isles's office and there was no
sentry at the gate. A group of men and women in camouflage
crawled along on elbows and knees, faces painted the color
of dirt. Their leader, a barrel-chested man wearing a scar-
let beret and shiny black boots, did not look pleased when I
rolled down my window and called out, "Do you know how
to get to Pukeko Road?" The commander walked, ramrod
straight, toward me; a line of sweat shivered along his brow
in the still heat. "Sorry for interrupting," I added.

The commander gestured with a board-stiff arm: "Make a
left where the road ends." His tone implied, that's an order!
Then he turned and snapped back to the troops, who had
lifted their heads from the ground, watching.

Isles stood in the driveway of a brick, 1950s-era one-story
home waving to me. As I hopped from the truck, I asked Isles
why he had an office on an active military base. We walked
through the kitchen and into the living room, packed with
tables and gift-shop wares.

He handed me a pamphlet detailing his employer, the Armed
Forces Canteen Council; the phone rang and Isles gestured that
he needed to take the call. The Armed Forces Canteen Council mission was spelled out in the pamphlet: to be the preferred provider of retailing and cafeteria services on all New
Zealand Defence Force camps and bases and to further benefit all those personnel associated with the NZDF through the
distribution of profits. . . . Their five-year contract with Antarctica New Zealand, the New Zealand government subsidiary that ran the Ross Dependency, began in 2002.

I flipped to the management board, all high-ranking military officers, brigadiers and commodores. Now they were
in the gift-shop business, too. Antarctic maps covered the
pale taupe walls, shelves overflowed with Antarctican books:

Matthew Reilly's thriller *Ice Station*, Kim Stanley Robinson's sci-fi classic *Antarctica*, Arthur Scholes's *The Seventh Continent*; and the gleaming, teal seas and curvilinear forms of soaring blue ice standard to coffee-table books, which rarely showed what the Antarctic often looks like, which is cloudy, gray sky, hung low, and all the colors muted in response. A subtle beauty and more realistic based on my experience.

I thumbed through the latest personal accounts, journalists, chefs, scientists recounting days of lung-cell-popping cold, revelations of women standing to pee using a plastic extender, and the same institutionalized histories, Amundsen, Shackleton, and Scott. The Australian chef's account found us in a remote South African base—I skimmed along and found her moment of falling for the married scientist, then shagging in a tent. No one knew we were shagging, she offers, as though anticipating our questions. Sure they didn't: At a remote tent camp on the ice, where about a dozen people lived? No television, movies, cafés, or bookshops, where in my experience you come to memorize every article of clothing worn by your colleagues because some days this is the only thing breaking up a view of ice, ice, ice.

I jotted down the book's title, *Antarctica on a Plate*. Someone had recently asked me when a story set in Antarctica would no longer be special simply because of the fact it took place there (driving a truck on the ice, making tea on the ice, sleeping in a tent on the ice). The answer was and is never— or at least not until the Earth warms sufficiently to make the Antarctic comfortably habitable. Until then, we marvel at our ability to survive in that landscape.

Isles, who had traveled to Antarctica fourteen times, called out, "Come see how I monitor sales down there with a quick call or a couple clicks of the mouse"—he could ring down there at any time and retrieve detailed inventories. Isles punched some numbers into the speakerphone. In New

Zealand, ringing Antarctica was a local call—in fact, Scott
Base was listed in the Christchurch phone book.

Margie, a cheery-voiced young woman, answered the phone
after two rings; she managed the shop at Scott Base. Two
cruise ships recently came to Scott Base, packed with tourists decked out in cash-padded snow pants. Scientists and
other field workers who vector through the Ross Sea bases
in force during the austral summer—close to four thousand
per annum he estimated—were the shops' nickel-and-dime
trade. The tourists represented a considerable spike in business: Ross Sea cruises cost about US$10,000, and the Scott
Base shop had no competition for their spending dollars.

The numbers he read demonstrated sales were up again;
two cruise ships had brought NZ$18,500 in business and
NZ$13,500 respectively. (One of the ships had been the *Kap-
itan Klebnikov*, with Baden aboard acting as historical interpreter.) Two U.S. icebreakers had been there at the same time,
which could account for some of the sales, too, he added.

Isles pulled up digital photos of the Scott Base gift shop–
emblazoned teaspoons, golf balls, Victorinix Swiss Army
knives, Traser watches, refrigerator magnets. Models of the
DC-3 (first plane to land at the South Pole), kids' daypacks
embroidered with penguins, spaghetti-strap tank tops. The
big loser came in the form of casual trousers that unzipped
at the knee, creating shorts—not a single pair sold. Maybe,
I suggested, shorts didn't offer the right sort of "I've been
to Antarctica" image tourists crave.

We took a virtual tour of the newly remodeled shop, which
resembled a hotel gift shop down to the Pringles and tacky
trinkets. Black knit caps had seen a surge in sales. "I decided
to add three penguins to them," Isles said, holding one aloft.
The penguins closely resembled chubby black-and-white
ducks. "Everyone loves the penguins," he added. "You put a
penguin on anything—and wham-o!—she sells."

I wandered around his cramped desk-in-the-dining-room office and noted a single page tacked up; Isles saw me squinting to read, laughed, and snatched the paper down. He cleared his throat and began reading:

2 February 2002
The aircraft was a Twin Otter two pilots, one engineer and myself. Nil freight on board, travelling from Willy's field to Browning Pass which is the airstrip used by the Italians.

We departed Willy's Field around 9 a.m. and we were going to a final approach at approx 10.20 a.m. I was seated directly behind the two pilots on the right hand side and the engineer was in the seat at the rear of the aircraft. There was a large bang and a violent turbulent shudder and the aircraft banked sharply to the left and in my mind appeared to pull up. The flight deck crew were extremely concerned and anxious, they voiced their concerns using explicit language to the engineer sitting at the end of the aircraft. He immediately jumped up to visually check all external parts of the aircraft. This was done in a slightly panicked mode, I was told to tighten my seatbelt and by this time we had overshot the runway. While we were circling for another approach the engineer was anxiously checking all external parts of the aircraft. The second approach appeared to be very turbulent and we overshot again. We did a large circuit in which the flight deck crew appeared to be trying to watch the shadow of the aircraft on the ground as they thought the nose ski had either come off or was hanging loose. As nothing appeared to be hanging loose we headed in to land and I was told to brace as the landing may not be as smooth as they would have hoped.

Isles paused and added, "You can imagine there were a lot of 'gee whizzes' and other stronger language being tossed around."

Then he continued,

When you looked out the window, you could see the plane's wing was blowing open and closed. If we kept flying the whole wing would have blown off the plane. The pilot had turned around and told me to take off my heavy coat. We all wore a lot of polar gear. We would most likely get soaked in fuel when we landed, so the pilot said there were two choices, if you get soaked in fuel, you're going to burn, and if you take off your gear you'll expose yourself to the Antarctic elements. I chose to take my chances with the elements.

"Hang on!" The Canadian pilot yelled and we literally fell from the air, unbuckled and ran from the plane across soft snow. No one was hurt, unbelievably.

The four men staggered over to the bright blue and red buildings of the Italian Terra Nova base; someone suggested they all get a whisky. The bar manager adamantly refused—the liquor stayed locked up until 6 p.m., base policy. Then the base commander came in and said, "These men need a drink." They spent the rest of the afternoon getting pissed.

Isles looked at the plane three days later, and it boasted new rivets and bolts; Princess Anne was due down to the ice and was slated to fly on a Twin Otter. When Isles flew back from Terra Nova Bay to Scott Base, a different engineer was on board. "The engineer remarked we were lucky the aircraft didn't cartwheel to the left, or the part didn't fly off and hit the rear tail wings, which would have definitely been fatal."

I asked Isles if this made Twin Otter flights to restock T-shirts and key chains less desirable. "No way!," he quickly answered. "All part of a day's pay!"

Isles detailed the planning of a year in Antarctic sales: "Think about this one: How do you estimate how much booze all those people will drink?"

I raised my eyebrows. I told him I had no idea what such an equation would look like.

"It's bloody hopeless! I have to order and have it containerized a year in advance—for people whose drinking habits I don't know."

"It's little things that can really bother people in Antarctica," he said. Isles articulated a well-documented Antarctican truth. Minutiae expanded in significance in the cramped, sensory-deprived atmosphere of a base or a camp, sometimes to the point of madness. Now, there was some stressful work—possibly running out of Jack Daniels and forcing a brand change to Jim Beam, a slight alteration in routine that could ripple across the community, instilling a vague sense of discontent.

At Scott Base, 46,800 cans of beer were ordered each year. A fax ticked in from the South Pole and Isles handed it to me. More beer had been ordered, but they had never heard of a brand called Speight's; the Polies needed to know, "Is that a 'dingo' beer?"

"Even at the South Pole they're ready to refuse Australian beer. Who wants to drink that piss, even at the bottom of the world!" Isles said.

For the next season, 2,268 bottles of wine were on order. In addition to Scott Base and Terra Nova Bay, Isles stocked Dome c, a base about 455 miles from the coast.

I calculated this must be The World's Most Remote Gift Shop. I had read about the scientific work carried out at Dome c. A recent report from an Australian group studying atmospheric turbulence said it was the best ground-based site on Earth for developing a new astronomical observatory. In order to compare to an optical or infrared telescope at Dome c, a telescope built at one of the next best sites around the world would have to be two or three times as large. Twin Otter airplanes were used to supply the distant outpost.

Isles ticked off the season's hot sellers, Pringles potato chips, penguin-embroidered backpacks, knickers . . .

Tryggve Gran bathes during the Terra Nova expedition.

"Wait a minute," I said. "Knickers?"

"Yes, knickers," Isles replied without hesitation. "That's what we call them. But you call them panties, right? Jockey-brand string bikinis," he added, made in China. Isles kept additional stock in the two adjoining rooms. Black, lime green, fuchsia, and purple, "Scott Base" printed in a white, whimsical font on the bum, panties piled high on shelves. On the next shelf four emperor penguins were depicted marching in a noble line across New Zealand Telecom's annual Antarctic-themed calling card.

"How many pairs of knickers do you sell a year?" I called out to Isles, who was back on the phone to Scott Base.

"Well, the core sales period is actually summer, when people come and go from Antarctica. In winter, the place goes to bare-bones staff during the twenty-four-hour darkness. So, summer sales? About two thousand pairs during four months." Isles sounded pleased.

As I drove out of the base, I saw the base primary school, and all the windows were coated with tissue paper snowflakes. Christmas in New Zealand is a summer holiday. Yet there remained an expectation of snow. The stacks of trinkets and clothing in the back room at Isles's office: Years, decades would pass, and the knickers would wander into a glass case somewhere. People would see them there, preserved as a sign from the past, sewing themselves into the blank space between now and then, a weave of fact into story into text.

Gently turning musty pages, Kerry McCarthy, Canterbury Museum photo archivist and Antarctic scholar, pointed to a series of photos of Tryggve Gran, Scott's ski expert on the Terra Nova expedition.

The photos held in place by black paper corners, making an album, a book, a primal instinct we seem compelled toward, creating a record of pages, rectangles of thick paper with a smell of yesterday. Imagine hands turning this page one day, in the sun, then tucking it back into a box, and sliding it under the bed. This one emerged from such a home. The people who donated it had said, we did not even know it was there, under the bed, all these years.

Maybe Antarctica's first nude photograph? In the immediate foreground you can clearly see a man's boot. Some might say the boot was included in the composition for scale, a common geologist's trick when attempting to explain scale of rock or landmass via photos. But I had to have the boot pointed out to me. All I saw was Gran's sinewy form, rising from dark, clear waters, grasping the hands of his Antarctican doppelganger, a balance of man and water and ice.

Field Notes

Eleven

We might as well have been flying in a bowl of milk for all the visibility we had.

      —Admiral Richard Evelyn Byrd,
        on flying in Antarctica, 1929

The DC-10 passenger has warmth and even luxury as he looks down on a beautiful but harsh terrain which cruelly tested the hardihood of the first explorers. He cruises in minutes over areas which took men desperate and trying days to traverse early in the century.

      —Antarctica: The New Adventure, an
     Air New Zealand brochure (circa 1979)

In 1979, 257 people died when their plane crashed into the lower slopes of Mount Erebus. It was and is Antarctica's largest tragedy and at the time, one of the worst air disasters in history. The Air New Zealand DC-10 had been on a "fly-over" tourist trip from New Zealand to Antarctica. This meant the passengers came not to walk or explore the actual ice, but to look down on the landscape and photograph it from the air.

There was almost no mention of it in any of the Antarctic museums; surely, I imagined, this would have to change. The event had dominated New Zealand news for more than a year as the inquiry unfolded.

Baden had told me most New Zealanders had some connection to a passenger or crewmember. The country was so small, he had reminded me, a disaster of that magnitude touched each of them.

On November 28, 1979, Air New Zealand Flight 901 left Auckland airport at 8:17 a.m. On board were 237 passengers and

20 crew. The journey covered five thousand miles over eleven hours, traveling south to the Ross Sea, where it would make an enormous figure eight over the ice before returning to land in Christchurch.

The flights had begun two years earlier, but due to facts of the Antarctic wilderness—no one flew during the formidable cold and dark of the autumn, winter, and early spring—only fourteen had been logged by Air New Zealand.

The plane was due back in at Christchurch at 7:05 p.m. An American pilot named Major Gumble had been forty minutes behind the DC-10 that morning, flying a routine resupply mission to the American base at McMurdo Sound, a huge annual effort dubbed "Operation Deep Freeze."

Gumble had talked to the DC-10 crew on the way south but lost contact with the plane as they neared the continent. As he came in to land, he queried Flight 901 about their flight plan. Again, he got no response.

Flight 901's initial silence caused no alarm. But when no one heard from the crew at several predetermined intervals, search planes were mustered. By dinner hour in New Zealand, panic began to set in. By that time, the DC-10 would have been nearly out of fuel. Something had gone terribly wrong. As the story goes, South Islanders had spread the word to switch on all outdoor lights, creating an islandwide beacon, help for what they prayed was a badly incapacitated plane limping homeward in silence.

At 1 a.m. New Zealand time, a U.S. Navy Hercules, flying in the Antarctic's twenty-four-hour sunlight, spotted wreckage on the northern slopes of Mount Erebus. The wreckage was a smear of black across Erebus's lower slopes, 1,500 feet above sea level.

In the end, 213 bodies were identified. In February, 1980, there was an interdenominational service for the remaining 44, and their remains were interred in a single, mass grave.

Peter Mahon had the difficult task of investigating the crash for the New Zealand government. Later, he wrote *Verdict on Erebus*, in a certain brave, frank tone. Mahon braided a clear map of the legal and procedural morass he had been asked to navigate. The obvious answer lay in pilot error, but Mahon was not prepared to accept this without thorough scrutiny of all the facts.

His diligent inquiry revealed the fatal mistake. The plane's flight-deck computer had been programmed with a different set of coordinates than those handed to the pilots. The plane was not flying the course they had reviewed in their preflight check. Thus, they were commanding a jumbo jet in the world's most challenging air space, acting on the wrong information.

In the Antarctic canon, ghoulish details packed the histories—a man made mad by cold and hunger biting off his own finger, dog companions shot and eaten as food ran out, a man urged out into the cold when his slow steps slowed the party from reaching safety. Something about Flight 901, though, revolted even the most enthusiastic consumers of Antarctic horror. What was it? The fact that they had been airline passengers, with no desire to even feel the cold? That all they wanted was to gaze down on distant snow and be home in time for dinner? Was there an innocence in their flyover, an innocence perfectly obliterated when they vanished in a smear of black across the world's southernmost volcano?

The Christchurch archives branch kept thirteen boxes of Erebus information, from passenger photos and brochures to the restricted manuscript written by the man in charge of New Zealand's chunk of Antarctica in 1979. This manuscript had been embargoed until September 2003, twenty years after it was written.

As I flipped through white binders one morning, a middle-aged man appeared who identified himself as the main archivist. He offered his help. Had I heard of the exhibit they had put on the year before, regarding Erebus? I shook my head.

He disappeared for a moment, then returned holding a spiral-bound notebook. This was the guest book for the opening of the exhibit. You might find it interesting.

A black-and-white photo of a cairn and cross and wreaths against a cloud-studded sky decorated the cover. The wreaths appeared to be mums or sunflowers or daisies. I could not tell from the photo what sort of flowers they were, precisely.

The notebook offered the chance to recall the day of the crash and reflect on how the exhibit reflected the event. Here is what was written on the pages:

Erebus Remembered
Flight TE901—an Archival Display

The display brings back the sadness of the crash and reminds me of the effort made to make the recovery successful.

This is one of New Zealand's defining moments and very close to Canterbury. Its sadness will remain with us for a long time. Very sensitive exhibition.

I still remember the stunned silence around Christchurch at the unbelief of it all

Great pictures. Sad scene.

Very moving and brings back memories. (All bad.)

Remembering that tragic event often.

Many more things should be shown of this year now that initial agonies have passed.

A wonderful father lost. Still very much missed.

Very moving, particularly the news broadcast the morning after. Incredible pictures of a tragedy that still casts a shadow so many years later. Evoked many sad memories of a very stressful period and the loss of a beloved husband and father.

Reminders of a lifetime lived without a father—Bryan may this always be remembered by us all and remind us of a country that pulled together, so I am told in a time of need. I love you Dad.

Well presented exhibition. I sadly recall having to collect up the possessions of USA citizens who were killed in the crash.

Remembering Jim Collins, Greg Cassin, and their families and all those who lost loved ones that tragic day. Hopefully further research will uncover all the facts and be on record as a true account.

The entries, so spare, read like something constructed by Basho.

I left the notebook and walked into the small gallery space, the home to an exhibit called Evidence of Us: Maintaining Today's History for Tomorrow. The exhibit space, the size of an average living room, was dimly lit and I was the only visitor. As my eyes adjusted to the murk, two views of New Zealand slowly came into focus: A map of Lyttelton in 1867 and an aerial photograph of what the crash of Flight 901 in Antarctica looked like from above.

A great clawed marking, black into white.

A placard offered this explanation:

What Are Records?

In the course of a working day people create, receive, or use records, data, and information of all types. The International Records Management Standard, ISO 15489 defines records as "information created, received, and maintained as evidence *and information by an organization or person, in pursuance of legal obligations or in transaction of business. It is this evidentiary evidence that differentiates a 'record' from 'data' or 'information.'"*

The aerial shot showed a dozen of the ubiquitous, tepee-like Antarctic field tents housing the recovery party lining the far side of the smudge.

Richard Evelyn Byrd arrived with airplanes in Antarctica in 1928. He flew over the South Pole in 1929, jettisoning emergency supplies to gain altitude to save his plane from crashing. This expedition, with its dozen huts, telephone communications, and modern radio towers, has been described as "lavish." On a later expedition, Byrd wrote on April 7, 1934, "The six month's day is slowly dying, and the darkness is descending very gently. Even at midday the sun is only several times its diameter above the horizon. It is cold and dull. At its brightest it scarcely gives light enough to throw a shadow. A funereal gloom hangs in the twilight sky. This is the period between life and death. This is the way the world will look to the last man when it dies."

Byrd, the exquisite aviator, had become a national hero in New Zealand, with his own looming shrine outside the capital city of Wellington. The explorer held New Zealand dear, and wrote of his love for the place in a book whimsically titled *My Second Home.*

Byrd, and all subsequent Antarctic pilots, knew you flew over the continent without any magnetic navigation devices. Close proximity to the Magnetic South Pole renders them useless. Pounded by winds, in a world where ice and snow cleave open, forming deep cracks, often hidden, fissures with a romantic whisper of a name, *crevasse.* More terrifying still the condition called *white out,* meaning to lose visibility during daylight. I wondered if those who conjured the term wanted something close to "lights out"—an order directed at children and soldiers from their rulers. *White out.* The Earth and sky as one seamless blank page.

In the archives, I sat down with several thick folders and began to read. The crash gave New Zealand an undesirable Antarctic superlative: Largest number of its citizens killed in Antarctica. An Air New Zealand brochure featured the white cliffs and frozen sea of Cape Hallett, stating: "It is unique among land masses . . . the world's highest and coldest continent, aloof, isolated, uncompromising . . . Antarctica. And quite impossible for the average person to visit until 1977 brought the era of Antarctic 'day trips' by jet. There could be no greater contrast between conditions met by those first into Antarctic seas and today's high-flying visitor."

The next week, I traveled to Wellington to meet the Antarctican poet Chris Orsman. He had agreed to accompany me to the National Archives in Wellington to review the mother lode of Erebus documents. From there we planned to drive to Byrd's monument, on a hill outside the city.

The plane lifted off into a hot blue sky. In the distance, the Southern Alps, a white spine of high, young mountains, glistened with so much snow. The clear, white light of it all.

The plane was an ATR 72-500 and two fat propeller-driven engines dangled from its wings. For some flights from Christchurch you had to go through security, but not for this one. This made me uneasy. How odd no one took off her shoes, or unloaded a bag. No, we all simply walked in a line across the tarmac where a cheery man named Bruce greeted us and talked about the fine weather. The crew wore black derbies and walked up and down the aisle with silver urns of coffee and tea.

Chris Orsman met me at the airport. He had traveled to

the ice in 1998 with the New Zealand Artists and Writers Program in Antarctica, and his recent poems centered on ideas of terraforming, Antarctic specters, while weaving in the histories of life in Antarctica during the early twentieth century. As Antarcticans who made sense of the place with words, we shared a specific dialect.

"If I could explain, or articulate what Antarctica means in a sentence or two, I wouldn't need to keep writing poems about the place," he said, lighting a cigarette as we drove along the colorful waterfront. I knew precisely what he meant. It was in this writing space, this place with no name but that felt like home, that Orsman and I convened on our shared obsession.

New Zealand was the first country to take artists and writers to Antarctica in a dedicated, annual effort. On their return, the writers toured the country, displaying and reading, sharing their firsthand impressions. Most larger Antarctic programs followed New Zealand's lead and established special grants for artists and writers, offering perhaps a half dozen artists two or three weeks in Antarctica.

"Who can quite define the Antarctic? The days of Scott and Shackleton were the age of potent myth," Orsman said. "You and I having been there have our own stories, but our own stories are stories of collision—we ram ourselves into these histories, like icebreakers. I am colliding with Scott at the moment." Orsman smiled.

I asked how New Zealanders considered their relationship to Antarctica. What else was it like in the world? "I believe you could say it's like Greenland to our Denmark," he said.

At the archives, we asked to look at the Erebus records. The people at the counter directed us to a series of binders, mountains of lists of documents relating to the inquiry and the crash. Then we were told that if we wanted to look at specific documents, due to their sensitive nature, we would have to write a letter to the chief archivist citing specific items and why we wanted to read them. I looked at Orsman. How could anyone discern the contents in any of the memos that were listed? It was all sorted by date and brief lines about author and recipient.

I then had a conversation with an archivist where I expressed that view, but I could hear my own voice getting too loud. The man standing on the other side of the counter looked at me with an expression that could be called suspicion, and then he suggested that my work around plane crashes must be stressful. I saw myself from his view. He saw me leaving the archives and catching the next plane for Lockerbie.

Orsman suggested we look at other Antarctic materials, and we found some film footage from the late 1950s transantarctic expedition. Men gathered in old-timey conference rooms, smoking pipes, looking at Antarctic maps. Watching those men look at the outline of Antarctica, hoping to draw in detail with their trek. I decided to follow their path. Choosing the best route by choosing the possible route and finding what is possible in planning and then in real time. We watched a few more reels and left the archive.

Orsman said, "There's something I want to show you," and we headed for the City Gallery, Te Whare Toi, across town. The artist's name was Rosalie Norah Gascoigne and she had been born in New Zealand, lived there for twenty-six years, then moved with her husband to Australia. She had been interested in ikebana, the Japanese art of flower arranging, then began scavenging dumps for materials for her collage-driven work, large-scale installations, many created from old road signs, which she used to create a luminous patchwork effect. Her work reflected on ideas of landscapes, how landscapes take hold of us, how we tell their stories. In one white room, *Monaro* dominated, a sinewy arc of sawn and split soft-drink crates, mounted on four enormous plywood panels. Where other Gascoigne pieces used

the words of the signs and crates to form the visual statement, Monaro sped across the wall on the energy of its construction, a geology-collage of wood in vivid golden yellow.
It looked like something forged by the Earth, somewhere
deep below the lithosphere.

We wandered back to his car. Time had slowed down while
staring at Gascoigne's work.

"Her work reminded me of the feeling of being in Antarctica," I said. "Monaro wasn't a collage anymore. It became
this place that was entirely other from itself." We drove to
the airport in silence.

Orsman gave me a present: A map of the Ross Sea region.
I carefully unfolded it in the car. The New Zealand government had issued it in 1956. What struck me was the vast open,
unnamed white away from the coast. "No names out there
back then," he said pointing. "No one had yet wandered out
to see what was there."

I looked at the scale, 1:4,000,000, and pointed to the number on the page.

"You know they have recently changed it from 1:250,000
to 1:50,000. The continent seems to shrink as the fine detail
emerges. One result has been a sudden demand for place names.
There's a Web site you can go to and propose names."

Orsman frowned. "I understand for New Zealand's Ross
Sea region, it's a joint U.S.-New Zealand effort, with the Web
site based in the U.S. I hope we can get some of our folks
recognized down there—I hope we can keep New Zealand
on the Antarctic map. There are just so many more bloody
Americans—you guys dominate if only by sheer number." As
I folded the map, he said, "Hang it on your wall and remember all your New Zealand Antarctican friends."

I combed through Erebus publicity materials on a final visit
to the Christchurch branch of the archives. On page 7 and

8 of a brochure, Mount Erebus was called the "Sentinel of McMurdo." Four photographs decorated this spread, two showing pilots looking out into clear blue skies at the nearly twelve-thousand-foot active volcano framed against the blue sky. One smaller photo showed a line of window seats on the jet. The four people pictured peered out delightedly. A gray-haired woman of about sixty wore flipped-up, snap-on sunglasses with her regular glasses. Her seat back was draped with a white, embroidered cloth. The caption stated, "Erebus, capped by a white plume, overlooks a frozen wasteland." Erebus is the world's southernmost active volcano, and a particularly unusual one, because within its ice-encrusted cone a seething lava lake works up strombolian explosions, routinely launching rock chunks skyward.

There are six photos of passengers in The Antarctic Experience. One photo features a man with a long-lens camera. Flight 901 was called the most photographed air disaster ever. More than six hundred rolls of film survived the impact, were processed, then handed over to investigators to study for ideas about what the weather had been like that day.

At the crash site, a group of mountain rescue experts and others had set up camp. A handwritten report in box 3, called "Recovery Party Report," was dated December 2.

> Arrived on site 3:00 p.m. Tidied up campsite. Began work on helo pad which continued till 9 p.m. involving five people. A sweep of the crash site was begun by the crash investigators and three assistants. The flight voice recorder was found at 6:30 p.m. After 9 p.m. the surveying began at 10 p.m. and continued on till 1:30 a.m. Nine people continued searching the crash and at 11:15 p.m. the flight data recorder was found. A search then commenced for the navigation computers.
>
> Work on the site ended at 1:45 a.m. and most personnel in tents by 2.30 a.m. (3rd Dec).

> *The weather conditions were calm. A number of skuas were*
> *observed attacking bodies.*

The next report, also handwritten, comes at 5.00 p.m. on December 2. It begins, "Skuas becoming a real problem. Pecking bodies. May affect your identification. Suggest sacking to cover obvious bodies this may require an additional flight."

Mount Erebus dominated Ross Sea vistas, drawing itself slowly up to 12,448 feet (3,794 meters). The notion that a plane could sled into it, because neither the pilots nor the navigator nor the landscape interpreter who spoke from the cockpit to the passengers nor any of the passengers could see it on a clear day defied comprehension. Overflying the Antarctic wilderness, they took along a historical interpreter, someone who had extensive experience on the ground. On that November afternoon, the voice over the plane's PA system was that of Peter Mulgrew, a New Zealand hero and seasoned mountaineer who had crossed overland to the South Pole with Ed Hillary in the late 1950s.

When one considers the number of eyeballs scanning the horizon that afternoon, the Antarctic's inexorable, historical trail of tragedy comes into sharp focus. If the best-known were the facts of Robert Falcon Scott and companions dying on their walk home from the South Pole in 1912 eleven miles from the food and fuel that might have saved their lives, all dying when one of their party seemed to have both the physical strength and the willpower to make it to that final bit and return with food and fuel, the final three men writing in their diaries as they lay waiting for death to overtake them, then perhaps the modern addition to this mythos was Flight 901, and photos snapped to the last second of their lives.

In another box, I came across an issue of *Skyway*, the edition of the in-flight magazine that was on board Flight 901.

A feature article celebrated the fiftieth anniversary of Byrd's achievement as first to fly over the South Pole. The article compared Byrd's flight, from his base Little America at the edge of the Ross Sea to the pole, a distance of sixteen hundred miles and sixteen hours, with that being made by today's DC-10, "Antarctic Explorers" traveling 5,360 miles in their spectacular day trip. The New Zealand flag that Byrd carried to the pole was displayed in the Canterbury Museum, home to the world's largest collection of Antarctic historical artifacts of this sort, that is, objects men brought with them, often with the specific purpose of bringing them back and giving them to a museum.

"Sometimes only three hundred feet separated us from mountaintops. It was nip and tuck all the way," Byrd eerily commented. Byrd's second expedition in the early 1930s was among the last of the great private investigations of the polar south. Governments were stepping in to make it their business. "I am hopeful that Antarctica in its symbolic robe of white will shine forth as a continent of peace as nations working together there in the cause of science set an example of international co-operation," Byrd once said.

Scott's story was told for all audiences, including in picture books written for young schoolchildren. In Antarctica New Zealand's library collection, housed at the University of Canterbury, I had found a slim, navy blue bound book filled with stamps once offered in boxes of a popular breakfast cereal. Back in the 1970s, children were encouraged to collect all the polar wildlife stamps and glue them into a glossy book whose text offered many Antarctican facts, including the deaths of Scott and all his men walking back from the pole. Taff Evans, the children were told, fell down and hit his head walking back from the South Pole. *Then he died.*

The Antarctican world presented as a narrative of scientific revelation. Questions posed, expeditions launched, and then maps and models constructed to represent findings in a fascinating, emerging world. The lessons of loss and human folly, the glossing, labeling, and building of glass cases filled with shelves to hold photos of the dead made more sense when those depicted were of another age. In Scott's day, a man who died in Antarctica could be simply heroic, an admired symbol of great human striving.

The story of the crash of Flight 901 performed something else entirely, a hero-less tragedy, the New Zealand cultural equivalent to the Kennedy assassination.

Expert testimony and analysis offered and recorded in the ensuing investigation: Professor Ross Henry Day, an expert in human perception, stepped forward to essentially discuss how people might not see a twelve-thousand-foot volcano in their path. Before he gave his opinions, he studied passenger photographs and the meteorological conditions at the time of the accident.

He said that the effects of white out are insidious in the extreme. Even on the ground the effects are not recognized by the affected individual until a gross error has been made, such as walking into a snow bank or falling into a hole.

But understanding what it means to not see in white out required a further explanation of a concept he called *the mental set*. What we can see in poor visibility conditions, he reasoned, was determined in large part by the *expectations of the observer*. Thus, as we scanned a landscape, certain aspects of it were privileged over others for more detailed attention. The final step, then, was for the observer to interpret the selected material.

To put it another way, we cannot see what we are not looking for, or when our physical means of seeing diminishes during white out, the mental set takes over. What we expect determines what we perceive.

Getting the crash site into order took until December 9. In one of the wrap-up field reports, a mountaineer who was called in commented on both what happened and how they did as a team; this document was titled "Report on the Recovery Operations of the DC-10 Crash on Mount Erebus." The writer had been in the Antarctic training a para-rescue team. What is striking about his report, which was largely created in plain language, were the mundane details of trying to live on the side of the volcano. Initially, they did not have enough to drink or eat. New Zealand's Scott Base staff began sending in cooked stews and water and beer. A Kiwi vernacular slipped in as the writer mentioned two days off the site where he was able to "get a good feed." He commended the high spirits of people working on the volcano in such difficult conditions. He questioned a film crew's access to the site, which did not seem to be based on what he described as a desire for a "historical" or "debrief point of view." He felt the media sought the kudos of "hot news," the money to be made in the sales of the films and argued all of this under the umbrella of the public's "right to know." The writer put "right to know" in quotes.

The writer also wanted to make it clear that the "tremendous job" was completed by a "cohesive team." This idea of a "team" doing the clean-up was considerably different from the spirited defense put into motion by the DC-10's owners, Air New Zealand. Considerable effort would be put forth to publicly blame the plane's pilots.

On the final page of his report, Mahon worries about darker times ahead, a future where the crash site would be viewed as "tourist attraction." "Anxious" was the word used to describe the mood about how to memorialize this part of the wilderness. Following the erection of a cross near the site, a long-standing tradition for roadside accidents and polar disasters, all flying into the area was closed.

The final folder of documents delivered to my table, an ivory envelope tied like a gift, cotton cord looped into a bow. Written in pencil on the folder, "Photos taken by Passengers 28/11/79 (Recovered from cameras found in crash site.)"

What impressed me most was the Renaissance quality of the cabin's arching beige passenger windows, one moment capturing a view all flyers knew, that of an enormous wing, almost impossibly keeping you aloft. Then the next shot was a view over mountains buried in ice. One creative photographer must have stood on her seat and aimed her camera straight down through the glass. We see the tops of mountains, flat white ice turning lavender as the photo aged, and the plane's wing: Information and documentation and finally, abstraction.

The next raft of photos was shot by Colin Monteath, a skilled mountaineer and professional photographer, prominent among Antarcticans, a producer of images that landed on cards, calendars, and coffee tables. He had been part of the recovery team on Erebus. There were two black-and-white contact sheets, with nineteen images, labeled "general views of wreckage," "whiteout," "wreckage," and "recovery team camp."

A man in a light sweater crouches among small, tangled pieces of metal. What happened, the investigations revealed, was that the plane was fully accelerating when it hit the sloping flanks of Erebus. The alarm sounded, warning the cockpit crew that they were too close to the ground, and then several seconds passed as they made the move to accelerate and pull the nose up.

The next frame was shot from a great distance. This one showed white snow, small pieces of metal strewn across the white, and pennant-sized flags on poles. *Flags Indicate Bodies.*

It must have been warm. In shots of men working, several

wore only singlets and stood leaning on shovels. A frame labeled in black pen, "white out." If I squinted, I could begin to decipher the lines of the tents I knew to be there. Or so I believed.

I looked up from this report, blinked several times, and watched a man in a green plaid jacket sitting opposite me. He was an expert on early New Zealand colonial history; one of the archivists had checked in repeatedly about travel times for official mail from Auckland to Christchurch via ship in the nineteenth century. (One month was the reply.) Behind him, a man rifled through folders, talking to himself and breaking an archive rule by loudly eating hard lemon candies. This was the entire population of historical researchers on one day in one archive on an island at the bottom of the world. I packed my bags and headed out into the cold, blustery sunshine. A southerly was blowing, Antarctic cold, leaves and bits of paper on Peterborough Street, lifted aloft on an invisible wave.

In April 2007, I stood in the Christchurch Art Gallery, in the second-floor room devoted to Antarctic art. A video flickered across the wall, a work called Black Hole/White Wall by an Auckland artist named Stella Brennan. The video offered brief, actual footage from inside the cabin of Flight 901 accompanied by the artist's ideas of Antarctica and childhood memories of the disaster and then some description of what sounded like a sad memorial built somewhere in New Zealand.

The word "disturbing" was in the text painted on the wall, describing what the viewer was about to see. After watching the work four times I was disturbed but not in the way predicted. What was disturbing were the words applied to the digital video, which ticked onto the screen imitating the rhythm of old teletype machines used by news

Field Notes

wire services. They would line the newsroom, each service—Reuters, Associated Press, others—with its own machine. The stories would emerge, letter by letter. I could see the day Flight 901 crashed, imagine how the story built from "DC-10 on Tourist Flight Late Arriving, Search Begun" to "Plane Wreckage Spotted on Volcano No Survivors Expected to be Found According to . . ."

Among the words on the video, this final statement,

> A performance
> A recitation
> A litany of lies.

This damning language came from the official inquiry. However, I wondered if she was also referring to her own storytelling about the flight and its investigation or reiterating the common cultural stance on the whole sad affair. Aren't all stories embedded with lies, creating a performance, simple recitations?

This bothered me in the same way storytelling around early Antarctic expeditions bothered me: It was the same way of thinking about the same events, even with decades to reflect on the whole affair.

The overarching theme of Erebus in its aftermath was a braided one, one part a stark declaration of the lies told, the other part a wounded sense of failure. Sometimes when Kiwis talk about Flight 901, when they say, "we all knew someone or knew someone who knew someone on that plane—we are such a small country," I feel it is code for something else. A sort of collective trauma and guilt. Like each person who lived in New Zealand in 1979 somehow had a hand in the deaths of those 257 people.

I had heard of videotapes shot by passengers recovered at the site, and those made in the aftermath. Bob Graham had been shown the Erebus crash response as part of his training as a volunteer fireman in New Zealand. It was not, he had explained, something intended for the average person. He recalled how one hostie, or flight attendant, lay dead, untouched, as though taking a peaceful afternoon nap, amid an utter chaos of wreckage and waste and destruction.

Lou Sanson had told me a few days earlier that the ice had vanished from much of the wreck and the Air New Zealand koru, its corporate logo, was visible from the air once again. The koru represented a fern frond as it unfurled its lush green for the first time and it symbolized rebirth.

A man stood next to me in the gallery. He said, "Life is too short for this," and walked out.

I continued to read the artist's words: There are so many ways to die in Antarctica. Why go there at all?

I was alone in the room so I answered the words on the screen. "Most people don't die there," I offered. "Most people go on to live their lives as they did before Antarctica. For some reason, a small percentage of us who go there bond and grow and integrate with the ice. For the rest, the ice of Antarctica takes its place among many stories and events and textures they experience. Neither more nor less."

There are more ways to die on the other continents, I reckon. Most people who go to Antarctica, who went in the past, did not die. Most got through it. Most prevailed. It is in our storytelling that we allow the dead ones to take the lead. We like Antarctica to be a place where there are many ways to die. But it is simply what it is, fierce and not designed for our watery soft forms. Go home, it says. Or stay. But stay on my terms.

Can facts only exist because we have a mental set offering us the material? Can I imagine more of place because I am willing to believe rational theories of place? Before fact, Antarctica generated as imagined Earth and recorded: Ptolemy and Pomponius Mela, reasoning perfect earthly balance, first described the existence of a terra australis incognita, or unknown southern land. Others added to the lore and ideas, including Marco Polo who reported a southern world glistening with gold. The rough Southern Ocean offers a spectacle of ice: bergs, tabular and pristine, not to mention ice fields, grease, pancake, bergy bits, growlers, swimming along with ships, as the sea rises and falls in cartoonish swells. A wilderness whose lethal presence refuses to fade in grandeur or terror.

Twelve

In steering a small boat before a heavy gale don't look back—it may disconcert you.

—Commander Frank Arthur Worsley

Navigation is an art, but words fail to give my efforts a correct name.

—Worsley writing of his work
aboard the lifeboat James Caird

In the New Zealand town of Akaroa, built by French and English settlers, a boy was born on a sun-filled morning in 1872. His name was Frank Arthur Worsley and he would sail all the oceans of the world. With mystical accuracy he learned the language of wind and waves and sky. In 1916, when Worsley was forty-three years old, he saved the lives of twenty-eight men in the sub-Antarctic by steering a small lifeboat across the roughest seas on the planet. That it was also winter and that they had already been trapped in Antarctica for three seasons and were half-starved, well, the tension mounts. When Worsley died in 1943 he was buried at sea by the admiralty, and lengthy elegies mourned his passing: the BBC, the *New York Times*, most newspapers in New Zealand and the United Kingdom, even the esteemed scientific journal *Nature*. For me, Worsley's story stands above all other Antarctican adventures, and his life, travels, and writings came to define "Antarctican." If the Earth's youngest continental culture needed a representative man, Frank Arthur Worsley was it. Worsley's

Antarctic adventures began when he signed on as captain of the three-hundred-ton, Norwegian-built *Endurance*. On August 1, 1914, she sailed from London's West India docks, en route to the Weddell Sea and the beginning of the Imperial Trans-Antarctic Expedition. The man who conceived of this trek was the formidable Ernest Shackleton. At this point, he had been twice to Antarctica and had made two attempts on the South Pole. After Amundsen succeeded in this feat in 1912, Shackleton cooked up an even more outrageous adventure: walking and sledging from the Weddell to the Ross Sea, prospecting and mapping.

Shackleton's bold plan called for two simultaneous expeditions, one to the Weddell Sea, the other leaving from New Zealand for the Ross Sea. The Ross Sea party would distribute a series of supply depots for the men coming across the continent. As they finalized their plans, however, the known world was crumbling. World War I broke out as they sailed. Shackleton offered to put off their expedition, volunteering ship and all hands for the war effort. A succinct telegram arrived from the First Lord of the Admiralty: *Proceed.* Winston Churchill had signed it.

On November 5, 1914, they were anchored off South Georgia. Twenty-eight men made up her crew, seventeen seamen and eleven scientists. In December, the *Endurance* slammed south into an ice-clogged Weddell Sea. By mid-January the ice had overtaken them. "The Weddell Sea might be described as the Antarctic extension of the South Atlantic Ocean," Worsley began his book, first serialized as a magazine story in 1924. "Near the southern extreme of the Weddell Sea in 77 degrees south latitude Shackleton's ship *Endurance*, under my command, was beset in heavy pack ice." *Under my command.* Who couldn't admire a man who begins his story by taking responsibility for their fine mess? Worsley's books on the *Endurance* adventure were published in 1931 and in 1940. The earlier book, called simply *Endurance*, recounts the entirety of the expedition, from 1914 to 1916. The small-boat odyssey was broken out from this longer narrative and published by Hodder and Stoughton in 1940 as *Shackleton's Boat Journey*. I believe a more accurate title features Worsley's name as the boat journey's architect. However, Worsley was an honorable man and Shackleton had been his best friend over seven arduous, adventurous years. Shackleton was the expedition leader, a national hero, and Worsley's commanding officer.

Yet Worsley concocted this single greatest feat of small-boat navigation, not Shackleton, and we have the paper records—the navigational logs, as well as diaries, to prove it. Shackleton was no navigator. The puzzle of it was how Worsley managed to sail a small wooden boat eight hundred miles in the dead of winter through ice-littered seas, a place for which the current edition of the region's navigational bible, *The Antarctic Pilot*, adds this caution: "all of the N Coasts of the South Shetland Islands . . . fringed by numerous rocks and reefs and should be approached with the utmost caution. Changes of depths in these waters are sudden and give no warning of approaching shoals. . . . The N side of the South Shetland Islands abounds in uncharted dangers."

Who was Frank Arthur Worsley? Worsley's character had been honed by the wild and free New Zealand hills of his youth. He documents this part of his life in *First Voyage in a Square-Rigged Ship*, a memoir published in 1938, reflecting on New Zealand's South Island and his apprenticeship on clipper ships.

Worsley recalled, "I was born in Akaroa, a beautiful little township scattered along the edge of the harbour and almost overhung by heavy bush. Before I went to school, at the age of five, I had somehow learned to read."

Worsley's father felled trees for a living: "Father used

bullock teams to bring timber felled on his run down the mountain to Akaroa. Eight bullocks yoked to the sledge in teams of four." Worsley then recalled how his father arrived home one evening soaked in blood after slipping over the edge of a steep track with his entire team. He reported every-day details of colonial New Zealand, a place dominated by rough immigrants prone to salty language.

"Several of these artists were runaway seamen, but no sea-man in his element ever equalled the profanity of a real bull-ock-puncher in full blast. One dear old lady—a newcomer—said: 'How religious the bullock drivers are: I've heard them praying half a mile off.'"

In a Huck Finn moment, Worsley and his brother sailed home one evening on a homemade raft to spare their feet a nine-mile walk.

"The harbour was three miles broad, and there was no boat crossing, so we started to make a raft of koradis, the dead flower stems of the New Zealand flax [Phormium tenax]. They were very light and made an excellent raft. We lashed bun-dles of koradis together with lashings of flax leaves. We then pushed a stick down the centre of the raft for a mast, and lashed another stick across for a yard. This we drove through the arms of our jackets for sails, one on each side"

They whittled paddles and at sunset, the boys' jackets filled with a fresh southeast breeze. "And we two Peter Pans dug our paddles into the sea with huge zest."

(As Worsley wrote his memoir, Peter Pan had yet to be adopted by Walt Disney. The boy who refused to grow up captivated theatergoers in London and for Antarctic explor-ers of the Heroic Age had served as particular symbol. Pan's creator, J. M. Barrie, had been Scott's best friend and wrote the introduction to Scott's posthumous account of the South Pole journey. Much has since been written about men drawn to early Antarctic exploration, men losing themselves in an icy Never-Neverland, including the fact that many—including Scott, Hillary, and Fuchs—named their sons Peter.)

As Worsley and his brother struck out for the far shore, the sea washed over their flimsy raft, spray breaking over the boys. When night came, they steered toward the glittering candle- and gaslights of Akaroa. The water was bitter cold.

Finally they reached the other side, far from their intended landing spot, and close to the most dreaded landfall: Murderer's Gully.

"This was a place where, years before, while two runaway sailors were counting over their money, one had murdered the other. We children were terrified of passing it in the dark. Suddenly, from the beach below, a series of blood-curdling, terrifying yells, shrieks and groans arose. I let out a gasp of horror and clung to Hal. Even that hardy youngster was scared for a moment. Then he laughed. 'Penguins,' he said, and on we went again." Not long after, they met their worried and furious father, received a hiding, and were taken home.

Worsley described his colonial boy's rag uniform, a cotton shirt shredded by tree climbing and work coupled with poverty. At night the men traded yarns and smoked pipes, drank tea or whiskey, while sitting on stone benches lining the enormous fireplace that dominated the Worsley home, a twenty-four-by-twelve-foot cabin called by its Maori name, *whare*. Roughly made of wood, the thin walls offered little protection against savage winds and winter damp. It was a smoky, shadow-filled room. Fireside tales filled Worsley's head, and it was perhaps here that he learned to be a storyteller and writer: "rounding up wild cattle in the Southern Alps, bushrangers, hunting wild boars, to tales of England, called 'home'—old Rugby days, school fights, fox-hunting, London theaters and "gals," Catharine de'Medici, Ulysses, the *Iliad*, Virgil, sailing-ship days, the Grand Tour, the beauties of the Rhine and the merits of their respective tobaccos."

Song filled the fire-lit whare, their faces, bronzed and bearded, lit by the red fire. "Larboard Watch," "Tom Bowling," "Home, Sweet Home," and "Rio Grande." Worsley recalled his father singing "Pop Goes the Weasel."

They survived on fried muttonchops, dampers of flour, water, and salt baked in the ashes of the wood fire, and stewed billy tea. They boiled their tea in the billy, a handful for each man and one for the billy. If a stranger came along, the billy was put on to boil again. At ten, Worsley was handed an axe. He felled trees, caught up in the sweet, rich smell of the wood chips, as well as the theatrical physics of trees falling. "The 'fellers' started up on the lower end of a slope, made small scarphs on the down and up sides of a tree. Working uphill, the highest tree was then precisely dropped onto the next one down, causing a domino-like effect. Often a score or more trees would fall this way, and I thought it a fine thing to see and hear them go sweeping and crashing down the line to fall in leafy ruin." (Of this clear-cutting, he would later write, "But it was a mad waste: the colonists in their greed for more grass seed and sheep pasture burned millions of pounds' worth of timber, recklessly destroyed the wonderful beauty of the bush, bared the soil till it was carried away in landslides, lowered the rainfall, and laid waste the homes of countless sweet songsters.")

Rain pounded the denuded hills, creating a yellow flood, running ankle deep. A half-mile landslide of boulders, shingle, shattered tree trunks, and roots crashed down the slopes, a creek diverted two-hundred yards from its original course. The landslide created its own howling wind and came close to burying Worsley and the rest alive. They had thought it was the end of the world.

Worsley's father took up bush felling in a nearby valley eight miles long called Piraki. Pronounced pee-rah-key, Worsley wrote, it meant "I love," as it had been a favorite haunt of the

Maoris. At night, his father played schoolmaster, teaching the Greek alphabet and Latin roots.

"For the rest, he sternly checked the colonial tendency in us to say 'taown,' 'caow,' and 'naow' and taught us to play the game and hate lies."

Many years later, Worsley detailed the environment of his youth: "black and white pine, shaggy barked totara and manuka, glossy-leaved broadleaf and titoki, the scented wood aki-aki, the golden-blossomed kowhai, the handsome lancewood, the sweet-berried konini, the fragrant-flowered currant tree, the ribbonwood, exquisite tree ferns, the common whiteleaf, the graceful matipo, the ironwood that blunted their axes." It was a dirge, "and the many other beauties of the bush found in no other forest in the world."

Wool moved around the coast from Piraki to Lyttelton, then onto the New Zealand Company's clipper ships. Down into the lower hold it went, above shingle ballast and casks of tallow. Only two weeks after shearing, the wool was speeding "home" in the clean-lined, American-designed clippers, the marvel of long-haul transit in the nineteenth century. Driven hard as any square sail, studding sail, and fore and after could drive her, Worsley noted, in response to the captain's grim determination to catch the February wool sales in London. His days working the land were to be fleeting. The sea would be his home.

On Christmas Eve, 1888, he bid his father good-bye at the Lyttelton quayside. *Wairoa*, named after a South Island river, was his first ship. Worsley had been a small child, but grew to five foot seven, 140 pounds, a man with a strong constitution and a sharp mind free from fear. Worsley watched as Dutch, Polynesian, English wharfies, with a polyglot of languages and cultures and dreams, crammed wool into the *Wairoa*'s hold. Then the *Wairoa*, laden with wool, sailed for London, a 13,500-mile journey. Imagine that moment in time: To understand Frank's early days at sea, it is crucial to first cast your eyes on the sexiest ships ever designed. An American conception, sleek clipper ships changed life in New Zealand. "Clipper" is a term often used loosely, but more precisely describes ships with a distinct shape. The wedge-shaped clipper bow was carried well forward over the water. The lines of the hull tended to be hollow rather than full, the greatest beam was well aft, and her sterns were rounded. Towering masts carried an increased number of sails. They were built for speed.

The era of clipper ships had begun in earnest in the 1840s, and the first arrived in Lyttelton in 1856. Experts concur that design refinements on these ships used almost exclusively between Europe and New Zealand or Australia brought the clipper ship to her last strange beautiful perfection in the New Zealand trade.

And when you lived on tiny islands in the far South Pacific, the time spent going to and fro was more than academic. Newspapers of the day gleefully tracked clipper ship speed like today's papers follow major sporting events. It was front-page news. Ships were lovingly described, "as beautiful a model as ever entered Lyttelton." The record for fastest voyage from Gravesend to Lyttelton was seventy-six days in 1871, by 1877 a clipper traveled from Lyttelton to the English Channel in sixty-five days.

The economic ramifications were enormous: faster arrival at market offering an edge on competitors. Perhaps more importantly, it meant the isolated, culture-starved settlers could get the latest fashions, magazines, and political ideas. It was a dazzling notion. The world was suddenly a smaller place. Goods arrived in New Zealand in the same time it took them to trundle by land across Europe.

This was the cradle of sea life from which Worsley sprang, and it has been said Worsley walked into the room like a gust off the Seven Seas, born on the crest of an ocean wave, cradled in the sailing ships, and exuding a tough and romantic character.

Worsley vividly recalled running down to Cape Horn, leaving the reader with the particular relief that accompanies not being there. "For some unknown reason, one enormous sea, towering high above its fellows, huge as they are, at times sweeps unexpectedly through the gales of the Roaring Forties, to circle round the world in the Southern Ocean, splitting great icebergs and smashing fine ships."

Worsley observed the helmsman in action. He wrote, "A helmsman in heavy weather should not look aft. Take a look at a mile-long 70-feet high cliff. Imagine that being hurled like a huge battering ram at 30 miles an hour at the ship, and some faint idea can be formed of the marvel of our escape."

By 1901 he was commanding a New Zealand government–owned three-masted topsail schooner, *Countess of Ranfurly*, a command that gave him considerable experience navigating among small islands. His biographer, John Bell Thomson, said that Worsley liked to show passengers what he could do under sail. Robert Louis Stevenson wrote in *The Wrecker* of a sailor who could put his schooner through a Scottish reel. The same was written about Worsley in an article on famous New Zealanders in a 1930s railroad magazine.

Writing to his New Zealand nephews from Rarotonga (also called the Cook Islands) on October 17, 1901, Worsley offered a biting, ironic picture of colonial life: "In this lovely island, where every prospect pleases, and only man is vile, the chief occupation of the white people in the island appears to be the delightfully Arcadian one of quarrelling, backbiting, and slandering their neighbours, varied in many instances with protracted drinking bouts.

"I am not certain of the number of cliques there are, chiefly because I am not certain of the number of white inhabitants, but I fancy they nearly correspond."

Worsley's letters offered yarns reminiscent of those heard in his Akaroa whare.

> Giving an idea of how these people have populated out of the way islands and emigrated from one land to another—A man who was nobody "kare o-upuapinga"—wished to marry an Ariki's daughter; but her people would not consent, and would have killed the man; therefore as they dearly loved one another and it was not good they should stay in Rarotonga, they hid a "vaka" (canoe) "e-a maro" about twenty feet long and filled her with "niu" (cocoanuts) and when it came to a dark fine night they crept away, put to sea and set their mat sail before the "Tonga matangi" (sou-east Trades) and sailed on many days and nights, till all their cocoanuts were all drunk and eaten, and from much hunger and thirst they fell asleep, and when they awoke were in a strange land called Manua (the Eastern of the Samoan Ids. 700 miles from Rarotonga) and the people were good to them, and their children live there to this day.— This is only one of many instances, and of course many more have miserably perished of hunger and thirst.

He records details of place with Thoreauian gusto:

> Aitutaki is a very pretty typical coral reef island. It consists of low undulating island a mile long, covered with cocoanuts and typical vegetation, with native huts built of coral blocks, lime washed, and thatched roofs peeping out in all directions, and a border of dazzling white sand round the island. All round the island runs a coral reef nine miles long, and four broad, on

the Eastern or weather side of which the surf thunders cease-
lessly in magnificent white combers, while the lee side is all
calm and peaceful. Inside the reef, the lagoon looks lovely with
every imaginable tint of green and blue.

While this Rarotongan command prepared him for his life
as a polar navigator, his prolific journal and letter writing
began to exercise his writing muscle, and in his life he would
write four books and earn steadily on the "celebrity" after-
dinner speaker circuit in between the wars in England.

Despite these writings, there remain many oblique aspects
of his life—for instance the fact that his first wife, Theodora,
simply disappeared while he was at sea. He never mentions
her in his memoirs. (I have been told this was the sad fate
many seamen returned home to, women got tired of waiting.) Or why he never tried to claim any real acclaim for himself, even after Shackleton's death in 1922.

Perhaps Worsley's amazing tale faded beside those of the
men who walked to the South Pole because most of us have
little idea what it means to direct a ship's course at sea. Walking, well, walking and sledging, even under the Antarctic's
extreme conditions, we imagine with tremendous confidence.
We may not understand the motivation, but we certainly get
the mechanics of it. Worsley's boat journey offered the inverse:
Any of us could imagine jumping into a leaking boat when
it was, so literally, the last hope. At that point instinct rises
over intellect, one imagines.

(Interestingly, the Antarctic was largely first explored by
seamen, and simple seamen at that, Baden Norris liked to
remind me. They were able to apply all the principles of sea
navigation to moving across often featureless ice, in a part of
the world where the magnetic pole hovers too close and a compass becomes obsolete. They were, essentially, ice sailing.)

Navigate: To find a way through a place or direct a course of something, especially a ship or aircraft, using a route-finding system.

It was and is a specialized skill. In modern times, the problem of location is solved by introducing radar, satellite navigation, the global positioning system, what is called GPS. Worsley's life as a navigator was based on three principles: speed, time, and direction, all calculated by his brain, trained since youth that if you err, you may die.

In the lifeboat *James Caird* he had paper, pencil, navigating books, a compass, a chronometer, and a sextant. All he needed was the sun in order to fix and record his position. The sky gave him this but one day during the entire journey. One day to get the path dead-on right.

I spent a day in Wellington with Worsley's only biographer, the author and fifty-year New Zealand news veteran John Bell Thomson. Thomson and I walked Karori Cemetery outside of Wellington where two men from the *Endurance* are buried, Harry McNeish and Thomas Orde-Lees, and as we strolled he offered generous insights into Worsley's life, "He enjoyed writing—in fact he was a very artistic chap and sketched and painted as well. Sadly his work went down with the *Endurance*, though one sample survives in England. Worsley wrote the script for an early talkie movie [1933], which he also fronted: it is an excellent presentation. The fact that he and his wife could live largely on the proceeds of writing—books, articles etc.—for some twenty years shows how competent he was, though there were certainly periods during which they were definitely short of a bob, and good friends were called on!"

I found in the Canterbury Museum archives a letter written by Albert Armitage, a noted Arctic and Antarctic explorer who first recommended Shackleton for Antarctic service under

Scott. Worsley had asked for Armitage's review of the script he'd written for the 1933 *Endurance* film. Armitage wrote back that while he found it entertaining, Worsley failed to tell the complete story, the story that would have portrayed Shackleton as a great leader, while revealing he was no sailor, and thus secured Worsley's place in history. "You were the sailor and thus the architect of the boat journey," wrote the great seaman, adventurer, and polar explorer, a man who had sailed with Shackleton, knew him well and had also been trapped in a small boat once in the Arctic and thus was in a position to judge.

Interview with Baden on Frank Worsley: He recorded this story for me onto an audiotape but would not allow me to sit in the kitchen with him while he did so. Far too embarrassing, he said. While he talked I took care of the daily chore: distributing one of many loaves of stale bread he got free from the local bakery to the many shorebirds that gathered in the canal behind his home.

I turn on the tape at home in Lyttelton. The persimmon light weaves into a sea of frosted mauve clouds. It is beautiful. The Maori call Lyttelton Ohinehou, the name refers to a young girl, hine, who was abducted by fairies, patupaiarehe, and changed into a new person.

> *Frank Worsley, born in Akaroa, New Zealand, is perhaps one of the greatest navigators the modern world has ever seen. And the reason for that is he served in the government shipping company and in the government lighthouse service, which entailed landing supplies at outlying islands, which naturally required great seamanship and handling of small boats. After that he was appointed the master of a vessel, an auxiliary schooner called*

Field Notes

the Countess of Ranfurly, and he traded around the Pacific Islands, therefore requiring a different form of seamanship and great navigation. So that when he was chosen by Shackleton to go down to the Antarctic and the Endurance he was a logical choice and he had many of the skills that Shackleton lacked. Shackleton had virtually no skills in an open boat and only limited navigational skills. I think we are all aware of the demise of the Endurance, the ship caught in the ice, the dragging of the boats across the ice and eventually getting to Elephant Island where it was realized that although the entire party could survive, they would not have been able to live through another winter on this isolated rock. So with the James Caird, which was one of those three boats, designed by Frank Worsley and then modified by the ship's carpenter Harry McNeish, they prepared for this eight-hundred-mile journey to South Georgia, the nearest point of where rescue could be affected. They overballasted at Shackleton's insistence and against Worsley's wishes, which actually resulted in a lot of that voyage, that very, very incredible voyage, being very wet, the men were very wet. Had Shackleton been a little less conservative and given the boat a little more freeboard that may not have been such a difficult journey. On that journey, eight hundred miles in perhaps the worst oceans in the world, one piece of equipment, one vital piece of equipment, there is no more important piece of equipment in polar travel than the primus stove, invented in 1896 by Lindquist, a mechanic in Stockholm, it is by no means an accident that both the North and the South Pole were conquered within a decade of it becoming available. It was the key to long distance travel in both polar regions.

In the James Caird was a little primus called the Little Comet, and it had to work. Had that failed, the entire expedition would have perished, not only the men on James Caird but the men on Elephant Island would have perished because nobody knew where they were. . . . We are fortunate to have

The Little Comet primus stove used by Worsley and the crew of the James Caird.

in the Canterbury Museum that particular primus. Harry McNeish the carpenter, who made the voyage with Shackleton to South Georgia, actually came back and lived in New Zealand at the end of the 14–18 war, and died in Wellington and managed to get a gentleman to deliver the primus to the Canterbury Museum as a consequence to being a shipmate of my father's many years ago. So in the Canterbury Museum, among its many iconic features, perhaps nothing is more interesting, and head and shoulders above everything else is that tiny Little Comet primus stove.

The tape ended and I looked out the glass wall onto the sky, and the curvilinear, snow-white clouds reminded me that the Maori had named this place Aotearoa, Land of the Long White Cloud, and it sounded like this, ow-tay-uh-ro-uh, with a light rolling "r."

Thirteen

Marston, the artist, assisted with alterations. Being stuck for something to "pay" her seams with, after they had been caulked with cotton lampwick, he used his oil paints finishing off with seal's blood.

— Frank Worsley, on sealing the Caird
for her journey to South Georgia

Unknown to known, the march continued, and the tally looked like this, the North Pole had gone to the Americans, and the South Pole to the Norskies. No one had yet made a complete Antarctic map. No one knew what lay beyond the shores. Maybe vast resources of coal. Maybe gold.

Thousands of eager volunteers answered Shackleton's advertisement for *Endurance* crew—military men, mountaineers, scholars, scientists, schoolboys, and a handful of women. In addition to sorting through all the applications, courting press attention, charting the trek, Shackleton raised all of the money himself—a large and under-reported piece of polar exploration history. He bought a solid whaling ship and christened her *Endurance*, after his family motto, *Fortitude vincimus*, "by endurance we conquer."

While the Ross and Weddell Seas cut similar wedge shapes into the Antarctic continent, disturbing its otherwise circular form, the Weddell is exponentially more severe—clogged with a fierce ice pack that extended 1,800 miles into the Southern Ocean. This ice circles the sea in a relentless clockwise drift.

Tracing the *Endurance*'s course, a course roughly resembling an outline of the human heart, you can see how they began at South Georgia, departing from the whaling station at Grytviken. From there, the ship arced south and eastward, past the South Sandwich Islands, crossing the Antarctic Circle around Christmas Day. They zigged into the pack ice in early January and were beset by the eighteenth day of that month. The ice, pushed by the Weddell's gyral, took the ship north toward the Antarctic Peninsula, also called Graham's Land.

They lived in a prismatic world, ice growing and moving by its own crystalline law. The water was so transparent they could see down twenty-five or thirty feet. The ice did not unsettle Worsley, or if it did he did not record this in his journals or draft manuscripts. Likely he knew nature, disciplined and chaotic, demanded first careful observation, then the ability to spring into action. He rarely mentioned the hand of God. Shackleton, on the other hand, carried a page torn from the Book of Job: "Out of whose womb came the ice? And the hoary frost of Heaven, who hath gendered it? The waters are hid as with a stone, and the face of the deep is frozen."

All of this captured by the Australian photographer Frank Hurley: They drifted for ten months northwards, the ship listed to the left, forced upwards, as though held slightly aloft by a hand from below. The images call to mind Edgar Allen Poe, one of his ghost creations, lit to gloamy creepiness by incandescent light.

As spring arrived, the pack cracked and rafted, slowly compressing the old whaling ship. The *Endurance* sank on November 21, 1915.

Life at sea is a collage of skill and luck, and the *Endurance* crew's life on the sea ice evolved into an amplified version of same. Hurley designed their makeshift stove, which consisted of a five-gallon ash bucket from Endurance, with a metal cup in the base holding methylated spirits, which when ignited heated blubber in a pan above it. Above this, another, larger pan then melted blubber, generating a fierce heat, which cooked food in a three-gallon pot resting on two iron bars. A piece of canvas stretched around four oars blocked wind for the cook. This tent filled with oily soot, coating the cook's face.

Worsley noted that despite countless new dangers and hardships, their spirits rose because "we had exchanged inaction for action. We had been waiting and drifting at the mercy of the pack ice. There had been nothing that we could do to escape." Their battle against hunger and cold refined itself over time. In order to sleep, the men needed to exercise to warm themselves. But too much exercise brought pangs of hunger. So a delicate kinetic equation was drawn, one that warmed hands and feet without exciting the gut.

I flew to Wellington to dig into Worsley's papers in the archives of the Alexander Turnbull Library. As we ascended over the braided rivers of Canterbury, the Southern Alps jutted sharp and cinematic in the distance. The third and final Lord of the Rings film would open with a parade that weekend in Wellington, and with little imagination I could see the landscape below morph into Middle Earth. I had read an interview with the director, Peter Jackson, who said the idea to make this film in New Zealand, the sense New Zealand was the perfect landscape for Tolkien's words, arrived when he was a young boy taking a train journey, reading The Hobbit. He gazed out the window and saw in New Zealand's thick forest Middle Earth.

The bowler hat–sporting aircrew offered hot tea from silver urns and a macadamia-nut biscuit. I considered Worsley's ideas on his quest as a stack of my notes slid gently back and forth across the small plastic tray, like a rising and falling ocean.

I made a list of what problems Worsley faced and how he tried to troubleshoot: Traveling with scant maps, he researched the voyage with the local whalers. In April 1916, when they set out in search of rescue, Antarctica remained a patchwork of sealers', whalers', and a sprinkling of explorers' maps. The first complete map of the continent was compiled as the 1950s closed. Sealing and whaling captains had culled together most of the information Worsley used, not an insubstantial understanding of those seas. Among the early records were those of Nathaniel B, Palmer, an American sealer who commanded the ship *Hero*. Palmer took credit for being the first to sight the Antarctic Peninsula on November 16, 1821, when the *Hero*, as part of a large sealing fleet, killed upwards of eighty thousand seals. The next year, Palmer met the British explorer and sealer James Weddell, in whose namesake sea (about 1 million square miles of water, putting it into the category "massive" as seas go) the *Endurance* went down.

(The plane hit the usual trans-Tasman turbulence. I no longer screamed in fear. No, as the jet began rolling and lurching, I simply turned my mind to the world in which Worsley existed. As he stumbled across sea ice, meanwhile, back in England H. G. Wells and other intellectuals were at work, their minds occupied with ideas mirroring those of the navigator: How we understand time, space, how we locate ourselves. Worsley, you could say, simply accomplished this in a more gut-wrenching, literal way.)

The Turnbull, in Maori Te Puna Matauranga O Aotearoa, was named for Alexander Turnbull, a wealthy New Zealand merchant who had bequeathed to New Zealand more than fifty thousand books when he died in 1918. Their brochure showed Turnbull, circa 1896, at the helm of a yacht with friends. I peered into a beige microfilm reader the size of a washing machine. Worsley's original manuscript lived in Cambridge, England, at the Scott Polar Research Institute, so I studied its ghost at the Turnbull. There's something mesmerizing about microfilm, and reading screens, humming along the reel, searching.

Worsley wrote his *Endurance* account in longhand, and I had become accustomed to his hand. In Canterbury, they had acquired Worsley's navigational workbook from the *Endurance*, a narrative written in numbers—latitude and longitude. Even without a ship to steer, Worsley had been responsible for minding where they were, how fast they were moving, where they might wind up. The log was covered in pea-green leather and many pages, brown and splitting, had been sealed in clear envelopes to protect them. Most of his notes were meaningless to me—noting planets' and stars' heavenly locations based on his navigational tables—until the day in November when the *Endurance* sank. Worsley had taken his pencil and drawn a sort of tombstone-like form around this fact—*lost at 69 degrees south*. I squinted at the microfilm. Worsley chose to begin by announcing his role in the *Endurance*'s fate.

"Near the southern extreme of the Weddell Sea in 77 degrees south latitude Shackleton's ship *Endurance*, under my command, was beset in heavy pack ice." This was the captain speaking: All blame or failing rests on my shoulders.

He quotes from his narrative log, from April 9, Sunday, 1916. They were stranded at 61 degrees south. *Stratus* and *cumulo stratus* clouds filled the skies. They set out in their three small lifeboats. "It is to be hoped the southeast breeze will hold and so save us from drifting east of Clarence. (Clarence Island lay twelve miles east Elephant Island. If we drove past these islands, out to the open sea, it would have meant the end for twenty-eight men crowded in small boats.)"

At sea in small boats, they feared the immediate, waves and ice conspiring to send their straining craft to the bottom. But there was another, equally likely yet more gruesome fate, which Worsley alludes to—if they miss his mark, they float into the abyss, and this death would be one of dehydration, slow, agonizing, maddening.

Large glacial ice has offered a note of terror throughout the ages—sucking in walkers, hiding dragons, shrouding mountains. For Worsley and the men of Endurance, Antarctic ice undoubtedly offered a curious beauty and on windless days a reasonably benign environment, yet their minds must have skated toward its menacing dominance and to recollections of other explorers' fates, the world of polar exploration, north and south, being literally strewn with the bodies of dead British sailors. For the scientists in their midst, the ice would have been understood through the investigations of Jean de Charpentier, Louis Agassiz, and the earlier writings of Horace Benedict de Saussure. Glaciers and the Earth's geomorphology had been the subject of lively debate in universities and academic journals during the eighteenth and nineteenth centuries and occupied the minds of both scientists and poets, with Percy Bysshe Shelley offering in 1816 that glaciers bore a strange magic. He articulated how freezing and melting ice destroys and reconstructs, grinding out new forms in the Earth's surface. Shelley and Mary Wollstonecraft had made a pilgrimage to Mont Blanc's ice and returned inspired by the ice's occult appeal and weird crags. Invigorated and inspired, the ice served as muse: Shelley wrote "Mont Blanc" and Wollstonecraft imagined a new world of creation, Frankenstein.

Worsley possessed the advice and firsthand observations of the Norwegian whalers they had met on South Georgia two years earlier. In those days, sealers and whalers were the most active mariners in the region and made thorough maps for their own use.

I looked at what Worsley had access to, including the early records of Palmer, the American sealer whose claim of being first to sight the Antarctic Peninsula remains a topic of contention. (The grim consequences of the *Hero*'s and other sealing ships' work offer one timeline for the knock-on effect of human tampering with ecosystems; in tandem with seal killing, whale killing devastated many species, and their failure to recover has left abundant krill for the seals. More than 150 years after Palmer, seals overrun sub-Antarctic islands where even twenty years ago they were almost nonexistent.)

Weddell, Palmer, and another British sealer George Powell, then discovered the South Orkney Islands, which Worsley and Shackleton would sail a northward arc above en route to their more easterly destination, the whaling station at South Georgia.

The *Caird* had been one of three lifeboats on the *Endurance*, the largest, and built to Worsley's orders in Poplar, England. She was twenty-two feet, six inches long, with a six-foot beam. The *Endurance* had been trapped by ice on January 19, 1915. The ice then slowly crushed the wooden ship, the inexorable push of gyrating ice pressing the mighty ship slowly to splinters. (Hurley caught this on film, and you hear the ship giving in to the ice, then a mast snaps like a tree limb in a storm, and ropes and boards making spronging and slapping sounds.)

The men then lived on the ice, at first attempting to haul themselves and their gear over ice ridges to land. This proved futile.

For the next five months, they camped on floating ice, drifting six hundred miles. Summer came, ten weeks when the sun never set and melted snow soaked their clothing. All the dogs had been shot, as had the cat belonging to the carpenter

McNeish. (The Antarctic life of this cat, a male named Mrs. Chippy, was detailed in a book published in the late 1990s. The cat has also been honored with a bronze replica in Karori Cemetery, beside McNeish's grave; perhaps this is one of the best-remembered cats of all time, and besides Shackleton and a few others, the most well-lauded of the crew.) They set out two days before Christmas heading to the west. Their lifeboats, loaded with a sledge each, weighed one ton. Dragging the cumbersome boats in relays meant walking three miles for every one mile forward. They could head for Graham's Land, three hundred miles away, or take to the sea and try for South Georgia, one thousand miles to the northeast. The ice offered chaos and tedium to their travels and forced many stops. Life became a series of precarious ice camps named Patience and Ocean. Spirits flagged but it was in these moments Shackleton's remarkable abilities to charm and lead and infuse light into the darkness met at a dazzling zenith. Worsley sketched in Shackleton's determination: "I have seen him turn pale, yet force himself into the post of greatest peril. That was his type of courage; he would do the job that he was most afraid of."

Their ice camps moved slowly north. As the ice floes broke apart, orcas cruised the open water, extending their mouths to reveal wide rows of white teeth. On the hunt, they possessed the power and will to break huge floes of ice from below. The men lived with hair-raising danger—drowning, freezing, starvation, or grabbed and pulled under by razor-sharp teeth crashing through the ice beneath their feet.

Five months of this have passed at this point in Worsley's account, and while I have read Worsley's book numerous times, I still struggle to imagine how one retains any shred of sanity when the world becomes such a hostile, barbarian place. Surely one must begin to feel abandoned, as though

God has left the world. Interestingly, many explorers describe a period of such thought followed by the sense that there is another, unseeable presence at their side. T. S. Eliot reflected on these explorers' stories in The Wasteland,

> Who is the third who walks always beside you?
> When I count, there are only you and I together
> But when I look ahead up the white road
> There is always another one walking beside you
> Gliding wrapt in a brown mantle, hooded
> I do not know whether a man or a woman
> —But who is that on the other side of you?

In the notes to the poem, Eliot writes, "The following lines were stimulated by the account of one of the Antarctic expeditions (I forget which, but I think one of Shackleton's): it was related that the party of explorers, at the extremity of their strength, had the constant delusion that there was one more member than could actually be counted." (Shackleton and Worsley and Crean told this story: All sensed another walking with them after they landed from the Caird voyage.)

In late March, the Antarctic continent was spotted—after five months of drifting. Worsley knew precisely where they were: Close to the same place where explorer Otto Nordenskjold had lost his ship twelve years earlier.

They knew provisions and a rudimentary camp had been left behind when Nordenskjold and his party were rescued. The camp was on the map: Rescuers might look for them there. Yet they needed to cross ice-clogged water to get to Graham's Land and the remains of Nordenskjold's camp. Shackleton said no, they would wait for the open sea.

One week later, the ice rose with the sea's swell. Worsley measured his time away from this motion: Fourteen months. It was his longest absence from the sea's roll since setting out from Lyttelton in 1888. The familiar rhythm invigorated the seamen. Worsley's mind was occupied with navigating. Ice drift offered a navigator maddening uncertainty. Shackleton ordered the men into the boats. Oars pulling against the swell, they set out into pure terror, seas jumbled with enormous floes thudding together, each moment threatening to catch and sink their small boats. Finally a dark line of open water appeared on the horizon, the sea reaching out a saving hand to cold, wet, half-starved men. They had broken free of the ice.

On April 9 they pushed off in their three small lifeboats. Their first landing was Elephant Island, in the South Shetlands, a remote, rocky, dreadful place that could offer only temporary quarters. Shackleton directed them to prepare the *Caird* for a run to South Georgia and its manned whaling station, eight hundred miles away.

Six men would crew the *Caird* when she left Elephant Island. Worsley and Shackleton had carefully selected them from the twenty-eight. John Robert Francis "Frank" Wild, the expedition's second in command, would stay behind with the remaining twenty-one and keep all hands alive and sane until their rescue.

Shackleton crewed his boat with men who knew cold seas—primarily from sailing and fishing in the North Atlantic. He also wanted to remove any men who might be inclined to challenge Frank Wild's authority during the dark, slow days of waiting for relief. The list of *Caird* sailors: Harry McNeish, the troublesome but gifted and resourceful ship's carpenter; John Vincent, the former bo'sun or midlevel crew manager, who had tried running the *Endurance*'s crew with a brutal hand but found his tenure short-lived once Worsley got wind of his tactics (Worsley then demoted him from bo'sun to ordinary seaman); Tom Crean, a strong, affable Irishman who had been to Antarctica twice before with Scott; and

Tim McCarthy, brother of the *Terra Nova*'s Mortimer McCarthy. Tim McCarthy was widely described as the best-liked man on the expedition. Except for Shackleton, all were sea-toughened sailors, with extensive Pacific and North Atlantic sea experience. They would call on all of this and their pure gut to survive what lay ahead.

Worsley knew if he miscalculated their course, they would overshoot South Georgia and be lost at sea in the South Atlantic. Death would come slowly, as they ran out of fresh water and food. Worsley knew that an experienced seaman could find a way to put this possibility out of his mind, could focus on the immediate present tense.

Certainly for all explorers' crews, the world is a place where you actively try to open doors, and you often open doors that lead to places not necessarily in the best interest of your personal survival. It is their job to invite the unknown into their lives; in this their lives mirror those of artists and scientists, to live on the edge of a dreamworld, to walk the line between what we see and what we imagine, to embrace their journey as an act of grace.

Amidst all of this ice and hysteria, as the men slowly morphed into a sort of frozen jerky (I gazed for hours at their photographs, wrinkled, blackened faces bearing an expression unseen in the temperate world) stood Worsley. He had to create a calculus that would take them across the water—a navigator of disorder, laying down his orderly lines based on the language of mathematics mixed with stars, a communication with the heavens and sky known specifically to him, a view that spoke to him in a most unimaginable way, dotted not with tonic blinking lights of stars and the odd planet but each light a signal or clue, like so much Braille for the blind man, ready to run his hands over the entire sky and say, *yes, follow me, I know the course.*

And so we begin the greatest story ever told, the greatest of all small boat navigations by a white man, and close our eyes, and imagine Worsley when he picked up a chronometer on Easter Monday, 1916.

Shortly after breakfast on that cold Antarctic morning, the sun obliged Worsley, and he was offered a clear enough horizon to get a sight for rating his chronometer. This device, the last in working order of the twenty-four with which the *Endurance* had set out on December 5, 1914, allowed him to begin calculating the longitudinal road ahead.

The other two lifeboats were used to ferry their supplies, including Worsley's sextant and navigation books. Then it was time to leave Elephant Island, a place Worsley wrote he had taken to pronouncing like "Hell of an island," to describe the Hades-like existence to which they had been reduced. How does one put into words the meaning of this boat launch? It was, so emphatically, *their last hope.*

On Hell of an Island, the men who stayed behind, led by Wild, three cheers were raised. As the small boat faded from sight, several of the men began to weep.

Their cramped boat had been overballasted at Shackleton's orders, which caused slowness, stiffness, and jerky motion, according to Worsley. Worsley had argued with Shackleton that a heavy boat would be a wet boat, but Shackleton, worried about underballasting, took other counsel. Worsley, of course, was right. Waves pounded the *Caird* and her crew, and soaked gear with frigid seawater.

I rang the Antarctic navigator and Greenpeace skipper Robert Graham and asked for help dissecting Worsley's work. Like Worsley, Bob was a New Zealand man who first went to sea as a teenager. When he got his master's ticket in 1972, a desperate shortage of men at sea meant Bob had his pick of positions. He chose the British Antarctic Survey and was assigned to the Royal Research Ship *Shackleton*. They spent four months that summer season in Worsley territory. Bob had made more than twelve trips to the Antarctic since then. He offered an insider's view of what it meant to take on those seas.

Bob, although midsize in height, cut a formidable presence, barrel-chested, fit, with muscular forearms. On his left arm a green anchor. He had long admired Frank Worsley and spent considerable time culling through archives, reading the peeling pages of Worsley's navigational logs from the *Caird*. When I told him I wanted to look through the specifics of how Worsley did it, Bob happily agreed. He arrived at my home in Lyttelton armed with navigational guides, his sextant, and a copy of Worsley's book. He had gone through the text and noted each instance where Worsley explained what he was doing.

Bob also came armed with many months of Southern Ocean experience. We settled in with a pot of tea in my top-floor office, a wall of glass overlooking the Lyttelton quayside. "I could sit here every day and watch the port at work, the ships heading out," he said wistfully.

Then he snapped his attention onto the matter at hand. "What you have to bear in mind is that these were hard men— Worsley, Shackleton, Crean, McCarthy, Vincent, McNeish— who had a healthy respect for the elements. In those days, the wheelhouse was exposed to the elements. So remember Worsley was used to being outside when he was on watch. They all were."

Nowadays, he told me, crews relied too heavily on satellite navigational devices, which had come into use in the 1970s.

"But when I was training at sea, we still spent considerable time engaged in the time-honored routines of navigators. We were told to understand every slight shift in the wind and how it would affect your course."

"Of course Worsley grew up navigating 'round Cape Horn on clipper ships, running in the wool trade from New Zealand to London and knew through experience the result of bad calculations, or misjudging the weather. Hundreds of ships sunk around Cape Horn, many without a trace," he said.

He spread out a map, showing the eight-hundred-mile boat journey from Elephant Island to South Georgia. He noted that Bligh, after the mutiny on the *Bounty*, had made what many thought to be the greatest singular feat of small-boat navigation. "The captain became with time the archetypal tyrant, but blimey, he could sail. But while Bligh's journey remains formidable, it was nowhere near what Worsley accomplished," he added.

"Bligh's small boat journey in the Pacific, and Worsley would have known it well as a sailor, covered four thousand miles in a boat roughly the same size as the *Caird*. Bligh packed eighteen men into his, Worsley had five plus himself. While the *Bounty* loyalists deserved their fame," Bob added, "Bligh had a warm climate and his crew were in good health. They could stop for fresh water. Worsley and his men had been stranded on the ice for three seasons. They were malnourished and had been pushed to the edge of despair."

In the back of Worsley's mind, he reminded me, was the ever-present idea they only had enough fresh water for a couple weeks at sea. "If they missed their mark, it would have been thirst that killed them all, I reckon," Bob said.

I wondered what made Worsley so confident that he could pull this off. Looking at the facts, their dash for help seemed only possible if one possessed the certainty of a fool.

Bob shook his head and smiled, then laid out the journey from a sea captain's perspective.

"Worsley knew what his little boat could do, which is more than important. He had actually drawn up the plans for the *Caird* and had supervised her construction. When they needed to modify her for the trip, he worked with the carpenter to make it right."

Worsley painstakingly detailed these modifications in his writings, adding fifteen inches to her height, building a whaleback at each end, and fashioning a pump from salvaged casings. When she was stowed and launched, she sat just two feet two inches above the water. It would have to do, Worsley wrote. (I later saw the *Caird* at a traveling exhibit in Wellington. The poet Chris Orsman and I were scolded by docents for climbing under the rope barricade and placing our hands on her sides. Although she's been restored to her pre-voyage state, making her rather boring to look at, both Orsman and I could feel the presence of Frank and his men when we spread our fingers on her small hull.)

"Before they left London, Worsley would have been flat out working out all sorts of contingency plans. That's what you do at sea. You need to know at all times what your options are," Graham added, sipping his tea.

This reminded Bob of a story. Once he had been hired to navigate convoys of crayfish boats to the Chatham Islands, a group in New Zealand's domain since 1842, about eight hundred kilometers east of New Zealand. (An interesting fact about the Chathams: They keep their own time there, so they are forty-five minutes ahead of New Zealand.) Sailing out into the great, blustery South Pacific the big fear, Graham offered, had been to miss the islands entirely due to bad weather and the inability to navigate it properly. "Bloody embarrassing, when that happens," he added, dryly. One earlier convoy, not under Bob's command, had done just that. When they realized they had gone too far, they radioed in for air support. A military plane was sent out firing flares, and all hands were summoned to watch for the light. The only flare spotted was also the last one the plane had to fire: Luck at sea. Had their luck been bad that day, the convoy would have sailed on eastward, run out of fuel, and all hands would have been laid bare to the windswept seas. "It's a well-known cautionary tale in shipping circles," he added.

Lost at sea has a creepy yet romantic ring to it, and I reckoned prior to satellites, it was more common than most realized. "Lost isn't the right word. I've been on ships where this is the situation: You don't know where you are. On the map. Lost and not sure where you are precisely, they're two different things at sea."

As I tried to make sense of this distinction, Bob explained the routine of steering by celestial bodies. The equations were all predicated on spherical trigonometry. You took star sights in the early morning, then did a sight for longitude later in the morning, at noon you figured out the latitude, then you checked longitude again in the afternoon, then ended the day with the evening stars. Each watch did its own calculations and charted the progress on a map.

"Worsley also understood the constant easterly current that forms a belt around the Antarctic as part of the Southern Ocean, moving in a counter-clockwise circle, around the bottom of the world. The water is constricted at the Drake Passage, thus increases in force and intensity, forced through a smaller space. This was where Worsley's understanding of local whalers' reports was essential. While at the whaling station on South Georgia, you can bet your life he spent all of his time quizzing those sailors about the seas."

In Bob's 1979 edition of *Shackleton's Boat Journey*, titled interestingly *The Great Antarctic Rescue: Shackleton's Boat Journey*, he had noted the pages where Worsley traced out his path using specific navigational references. Navigation was and is a specialized skill. The central ingredients in finding your way, speed, time, and direction.

In the lifeboat *James Caird* Worsley had paper, pencil, navigating books, a compass, a chronometer, and a sextant. All he needed were celestial bodies in order to fix and record his position. Bob talked about another crucial navigating tool: Dead reckoning.

The word *dead*, he assured me, had no morbid associations. No, it was derived from the abbreviation "ded" for deduced. To navigate by what seamen call DR you deduce a new position from an earlier one using on-board measurements of speed and direction. However, he noted, this can be tricky even in the best of circumstances, which the Antarctic does not offer. Small, persistent errors accumulate.

Yet, he added, Worsley was undoubtedly a sailor who could tell his boat's speed, most likely to within half a knot, from the sails.

"Never forget his clipper ship training," he added. This was how he understood the seas, not by engine speed but by sail speed.

Worsley, however, commented in the book that his DR often fell wide of the mark: "In the dark our course was most erratic, and at all hours the iron rod of the pump was working up and down within a few inches of the compass." He offers the plain facts, the lack of candlelight to see the compass, the endlessly soaking waves, hands frozen to the oars, deerskin sleeping bags disintegrating in sloggy seawater, hair working its way into every beverage and hot cup of gruel.

He saw the moon only once on the entire journey. He called his work, "grin and bear it time."

What he faced: "From 55 degrees to 60 degrees of latitude south is the battleground of two great wind systems—the circumpolar westerlies and the polar easterlies; but around Elephant Island the westerlies are forced farther south by the thrust and direction of the Andes Mountains and Cape Horn." He knew these winds meant there was no hope of reaching Cape Horn. They had to aim for South Georgia. Huge waves, howling winds, and the ever-present possibility of broaching.

"What's broaching?" I asked Bob.

"It's when seas are coming astern. You lose steerage and go side on to the sea and you tend to roll over." Bob raised his gray eyebrows. Worsley had to think about who could handle this, day in and day out. "You know, he writes very eloquently about how you are taught at sea to never look behind you," Bob said.

"Why's that?" I wondered.

"Because it's bloody scary! To see this ginormous thing coming towards you. That's when you begin to wonder why you didn't become a farmer." He paused and gazed out to the port where a gray freighter stacked with orange and green containers took in fuel before heading out into the Pacific. "Of course it's exhilarating at the same time."

We studied the map of Worsley's boat journey. "You know, the sky never gave him a break during those sixteen days. He rarely had anything but a solid ceiling of gray clouds. This wasn't unusual for down there. It can go on like that for bloody weeks. And it was late in the summer season."

The only good time to take a ship into the Antarctic, he reminded me, was summer when the ice broke up and the weather warmed slightly. Worsley was now stuck with pushing off in the small boat in late April, winter loomed. He wrote this grim pronouncement, *the southern winter was upon us.* Starving, frozen, demoralized men, a small wooden boat overballasted and offering a wet ride, ice and wind and reindeer hair from their soaked sleeping bags infiltrating their water and food.

(In the Akaroa Museum, not far from where Worsley was born, I held Worsley's notebooks, wearing thin white cotton gloves. Handwritten, one long-take fountain pen on lined pages, he outlined the events of his books, set a course, followed it. He unraveled a story of what it means to understand wind, water, sky, how to travel from one place to another in a small wooden boat of one's own design. I wept, amidst stacks of old newspapers and a handful of cardboard boxes holding ephemera from Worsley's life, objects yet to be woven into their single glass case capturing his life.)

Worsley's pea-green leather log of the *Caird* journey offers his handwriting during these days at sea; it expands and wavers as he scratches out the days. Navigational tables abound, lines and lines of calculations. Math offering a set language for where they were heading. In this same journal, he created maps of anchorages they found when they arrived at South Georgia and sailed into a small bay named for Norway's King Haakon. As a South Pacific sailor, Worsley knew how to land small boats in rough seas on steep beaches. Yet the harrowing moments he documents, so close to land, so perilous to get ashore, so desperate for fresh water, made me wonder why he took time to draw maps when they were so close to dying. Bob explained simply that all seamen make maps. "Even today, each Antarctic trip offers fresh or unknown information about how the land or seascape works. There's always something new to learn about the wild. You jot it down so you can tell your mates, other sailors and skippers. To help them out should they find themselves in the same spot one day. We all look out for one another. And you never consider it's your last day. Worsley would not have been thinking, 'I wonder if it makes sense to make maps when I am about to die.' It's just not the way we think at sea," he added.

Shackleton and Worsley would make four attempts over as many months before successfully rescuing the Elephant Island group. They had survived under the two remaining lifeboats, fashioning hammocks to accommodate all the men, eating seals. When their youngest member, a stowaway named

Perce Blackborrow suffered the agony of blackened, infected, frostbitten toes, they cut them off and saved his life. Worsley, Shackleton and the rest then headed for South America, to a hero's welcome in Chile. Then the crew departed for England and the Great War, and Shackleton and Worsley set off for New Zealand, via New Orleans and San Francisco. They had to bring back their Ross Sea party, still stranded in Antarctica. Worsley used to say about his Antarctic explorations with Shackleton, of the years they spent exploring side by side, that they did the most dangerous things but did them in the safest way.

Worsley's feat, lauded to this day as Shackleton's triumph, was aptly described by Captain H. Taprell Dorling, DSO, RN, as one difficult to read about without feeling the thrill of admiration for those who accomplished it.

Yet it is in the details of Worsley's vivid accounts that the story has come to occupy my mind, not as a superlative nor as action judged and rated by fellow seamen or historians. I cast my mind back over his words. By the end of the journey, their hands were raw and bleeding from crawling over the rock ballast in the boat. Their thighs rubbed raw by wet clothing. Shackleton in acute pain with sciatica. Salt water broached their fresh water. Reindeer hair in each sip and bite. Each salty sip made them thirstier. Tongues and lips swelled. As they approached South Georgia, a huge tempest caught them and nearly drove them with the speed of a freight train into a towering wall of rock. Worsley ordered them to set the reefed jib and the mizzen. He battled the wind with his ragged sails. One man and some pieces of fabric to ensure twenty-eight would live. What he thought in those final battles before reaching shore, in a rare moment of discouragement: *What a pity. We have made this great boat journey and no one will ever know.*

Explorers tolerate their missteps as part of their wanderings, an unusual mixture of precision in mapping a course and a tolerance, or appetite, for letting go. Maybe the word was *disappear*, not lost. A tolerance to vanish and reappear; not everyone can stomach erasing herself, and in these times it feels as though we tolerate this disconnect less and less. (At the market, I wait in line with women in the express lane, buying ivory parsnips, shiny fennel, organic carrots. Each clutches a mobile phone, and the phones ring and they press a button and they are tracked by a global positioning system. They walk out of the store, phones pressed to ears. Known and connected and part of some perceived Web.)

I was curious about getting *lost* at sea. "It's not that they were lost, in the way people on shore use the word. It's just that you don't know precisely where you are. They're two different things at sea." At sea, the sky points the way across the Earth's surface, a path of planets and stars, of angles, of horizon. Later, satellites winking along would tell the same story, and clicking and whirring machines on the ship's bridge marking a trail.

These conditions, which only become more hideous as the details were revealed, actually begin to point to what prompted Worsley to write this book in the first place. Why did he write that book? Handwritten, one long-take fountain pen on lined pages? He knew in his day the triumph of Shackleton was the preeminent goal. But I believe he knew something else. That by putting pen to paper in 1916, he telegraphed something else to the future. He was sending us a message about what it means to understand wind, water, sky. He was telling us how to travel from one place to another in a small wooden boat of one's own design. As a Pacific sailor, he knew of Bligh. As a skilled navigator, he knew what he had pulled off during those sixteen days. He knew that he had made the world's greatest small boat journey. As a man who had been reared in the wilds of a volcano's maw, he knew the value of understanding how to place yourself in a landscape. It is a book about living in the absolute present tense. A book that teaches us many small lessons, the importance of each day, a hot cup of tea, and courage to never look behind you.

The writer Patrick O'Brian noted in a later edition's preface that Worsley "possessed a highly developed aesthetic sense and he was deeply moved by the extraordinary beauty of Polar color, its clarity, its prismatic brilliance in the more-than-frozen air, the unimaginable beauties of the ice, of tumbled, shattered pack-ice and of majestic bergs, large as half the county."

As the clouds collapsed on a cold summer day in Lyttelton, I found Frank, so clear and true, as though he sat with me on the borrowed leather sofa. Yes, he seemed to say, yes this is how the real world goes. Watch the skies, spend each day outdoors, and never be afraid to face down the weather. *And don't look back.*

Field Notes

Here's one story about penguins: Once they choose a partner, they do so for life. They mate once a year in the fall. The female is on her stomach on the ice, face down, the male lies on top of her. It's all over in ten seconds.

Yet more recent reports suggest penguins don't live this way at all; no, in this report we hear of all sorts of eyebrow-raising behavior, nest hopping, homosexuality. Not to mention the well-documented egg-stealing that goes on. Models of what political conservatives mean when they discuss "family life," or something quite the contrary?

I imagine if penguins were to study us the way we study them, they might be intrigued by how we adapt to and construct our habitats. Maybe they would investigate our habitat construction in places like New York. How we stack boxes of stone one on top of the other and then argue among ourselves about what color the inside of these dens should be. How we change the den's color randomly. Or do we do so for other reasons? Perhaps, as scientists do in the Antarctic, they would be curious about whether or not helicopter noise disrupted our breeding habits. Penguins may be the most carefully studied of all Antarctic wildlife, and there was a lot of grumbling among Antarctic scientists about duplication and relevance. Yet penguins hold our attention in ways seals do not. Why is this so? And why do we insist on making them into comical little men in dinner suits, carrying silver trays of Champagne? Baden had run a bird "hospital" for many years. As part of this, he had worked with the indigenous species called the blue or little penguin, Eudyptula minor. (The Maori name is korora, and it is the world's smallest penguin. This penguin weighs about 1 kilo, or 2.2 pounds, and stands no more than 25 centimeters high.) These penguins have suffered from gruesome predation, and introduced species like ferrets, stoats, weasels, house cats, and the family dog make fast work of them. Among those in his care was a penguin that had arrived with a damaged bill and one blind eye. Baden named him Percy and said he never could have survived again in the wild. While he lived with Baden, Percy got to know Baden's cats, who came to treat the little bird with respect and accepted him as part of the household. Baden explained how other penguins were in hospital because they had become oil contaminated. To cure them, Baden gave them detergent baths, then carefully checked that all residue was removed. After about five weeks, most were ready to be reintroduced to the wild. They usually did not want to go, he added. He recalled one particular day when he had four to release, how he took them down to the beach and shooed them all toward the sea, then sat on the beach and watched them swim away. One by one, they came back to the beach and sat down next to him. Then the five watched the surf roll onto the beach at Sumner. Two penguins tired of this, and wandered back toward the waves, but the other two were quite determined to come home with Baden. So Baden brought them to the beach again the next day, and this time only one turned from the waves. A few days later he, too, agreed to swim out to sea. Returning to the sea was no longer an option for Percy. He came to have a taste for cat food and enjoyed daily swims with Baden in the surf. Percy rode to the beach in the boot, or trunk, of Baden's white car. When they finished their swim, Percy waddled back to the car park. "He always knew which car was ours, he was a smart penguin," Baden recalled. I pictured the two of them rolling in the turquoise South Pacific waters. So Percy lived his half-penguin, half-human life making a comfortable nest in the cold furnace in the basement. During one of the South Island's torrential rainstorms, he was molting, and water surged into his molting area, and by the time Baden found him, he was ice-cold and water-logged. Wrapped in shawls and held tight, Percy died. Down the coast from Baden's home, many years later, the town of Oamaru became home to a set of wooden burrows and bleachers, a habitat restoration project with spectators, where tourists paid to watch penguins emerge from the sea as night descended. They hopped up the rocky beach. When we visited, one turned toward where I sat with my children and came to within a few feet of us, looking steadily at our family. Then the penguin turned toward the hills and began to climb toward the burrows. In the gift shop, we bought small plastic replicas of the little blue penguins. They were made in China and stood as tall as my thumb.

Fourteen

Ko au te awa, ko te awa ko au—*I am the river, the river is me.*

Nature is the receptacle which contains man and into which he finally sinks to rest. It implies all that man knows or can know.

—Loren Eiselcy

Never lose sight of the ultimate goal, and focus energy on short-term objectives. . . . Set a personal example with visible, memorable symbols and behaviors. . . . Instill optimism and self-confidence, but stay grounded in reality. . . . Take care of yourself: Maintain your stamina and let go of guilt. . . . Reinforce the team message constantly: "We are one—we live or die together."

—Graduate business schools now deploy
Shackleton's polar ethos to teach the next
generation of business leaders how to lead

It is April and I am about to set myself free. I sit in Bryan Storey's office at Gateway Antarctica and listen as he discusses global climate change. While I listen, I hold and read a paper titled "The Antarctic and Climate Change," compiled by the Antarctic and Southern Ocean Coalition, based in Washington DC. (Scientists tell the story of how our Earth's shifting climate will be seen in changing weather patterns, framing this discussion with the distinction between climate and weather—climate being patterns of weather observed over time, weather being storms, sunshine, barometric pressure—how the discussion centers on locating techniques to measure changes people have yet to imagine. A fresh set of variables to list, sort, collect data on, consider, mull, ponder, then report.) Just when the entire planet is mapped, when we think seriously about travel to Mars, we find there is a new Earth to explore. What sort of Earth will this be, you might ask? This is a question no one can answer but rests over a denominator of certainty.

I ask Bryan to sum it all up, to put all the facts of climate change into a sentence or two. "This is the story: It is amazing that human beings, with our little fires, have affected the Earth's composition to the point where the atmosphere has been altered."

Bryan continues to talk, pulls newspaper clippings from files. My eyes wander across the pages, "Antarctica comprises two geologically distinct regions, East and West Antarctica, separated by the Transantarctic Mountains but joined together by an all-encompassing ice sheet. The presence of the high ice sheet and the polar location make Antarctica a powerful heat sink that strongly affects the climate of the whole Earth. Furthermore, the annual sea ice cover around the continent, which seasonally reaches an area greater than that of the continent itself, modulates exchanges of heat, moisture, and gases between the atmosphere and ocean. As the sea ice forms each winter, the salt it rejects sinks to the sea floor to form cold, dense oxygen-rich Antarctic Bottom Water that flows north under the world's oceans, driving the 'ocean conveyor' and ventilating deep-sea life."

I pause in my reading as Bryan sits down across from me. First, he shows me a profile from the BBC of the U.K. Chair of Shell, Lord Ronald Oxburgh. What strikes is the first paragraph, noting he has made a name for himself because of public worrying over the effects of greenhouse gases and the problem of climate change. He is quoted as saying, "There is little hope for the world" unless carbon dioxide emissions are dealt with. Then Bryan pulls out the latest report from the Intergovernmental Panel on Climate Change, a report referred to as an assessment, the fourth in a series. In this fourth, they introduce the word "unequivocal" to describe evidence that humans are to blame for the warming Earth. (I have seen this feeling quantified: that is, now that the numbers are in, we are 90 percent certain we are to blame. But the IPCC is consensus driven and thus hurls out any science considered controversial, or not yet incorporated into current climate models or not fully articulated in numbers. So skeptics, like those who pepper the news whenever debates are performed on television networks, muddying the waters with doubt, a doubt many want to hold onto like man and preserver overboard, *surely all this is some nightmarish glitch*, continue to be pushed to discussion's edge, although in the United States, alarmingly, they often get equal time.) Yet in this unanimity of opinion they also pushed to the rear science suggesting that we are speeding, zooming, going at light speed toward a new Earth. I think, well, it solves the question about whether we need to explore Mars. Who needs to go poking around in outer space when we get a whole new planet under our feet? A new list: a collapsing Greenland ice sheet, a shut-down of the Gulf Stream, carbon dioxide and methane released from the soil and the ocean bed, and melting permafrost, and of course, Antarctica a shattered patchwork of ice. No longer smooth, wind ripping giant ice glowing like a beacon into the cosmos. Could Antarctica's huge ice sheets be close to disintegration? If this happened, sea level would rise in meters, not the centimeters per year reported by the IPCC.

One of the concerns, Bryan said, is that current models assume ice sheets will melt only slowly, but many glaciologists no longer believe this is what will happen. These glaciologists, he explained, have observed that ice sheets fracture as they melt, allowing water to penetrate to the bottom of the ice within seconds, effectively lubricating along the bedrock where it rests. Thus, melting is not the only concern with ice sheets. Scientists are also looking at what happens when the ice physically breaks up.

"Once some changes are set in motion," he added, "it will not matter what happens with CO_2 emissions."

For instance? I ask.

"Well, in Antarctica, the East Antarctic Ice Sheet sits on land. However the West Antarctic Ice Sheet rests primarily on a part of the continental shelf that is below sea level. As early as the late 1970s, researchers indicated this fact might make the West Antarctic ice sheet particularly prone to collapse. If this entire ice sheet slides off the continental shelf, bit by bit, global sea level will rise five meters whether the ice melts or not." In models of what this means geographically, the lowest third of Florida, including Miami, is under water.

Other scientists tell stories of world sea levels rising 50 percent faster than predicted in the third IPCC report, published in 2001. Bryan looks around the room and says, "Do you remember the film, *The Day After Tomorrow*? Surprisingly, that was reasonable science, showing the closing down of the North Atlantic Drift. Scientists have been studying that possibility for some time. They believe the Gulf Stream slowed by close to 30 percent between 1957 and 2004. How the world's oceans circulate and the result of any changes to these patterns are often discussed by scientists in the context of this question: What happens if these conveyor belts of ocean currents, or lapping air patterns, shut down? Huge and unpredictable repercussions for world climate."

The climate story and its facts are predicated on information that can be quantified. Qualitative storytelling doesn't cut much ice around serious scientists. No one wants someone running around with a hunch about the climate, or so it seems. But some days I do. Some days I miss those doctrinaire Greenpeace sessions, afloat in the Ross Sea, where everyone was so sure the Antarctic could be saved from commercial development if we just took enough pictures, wrote the right stories, gathered enough effluent. The point was action, or a decision not to ride with inaction, the point was to feel some agency as a person alive on this planet, Antarctican,

or not, or as Frank Worsley might have added, not on my
bloody watch.

Cold, cold water surrounds me. I recall a scene from The Day
After Tomorrow, a film that completely and perfectly freaked
me out, when a large wave rolls through Manhattan, smashing everything in its path, and as the water begins its chaotic surge, cars and people jam the streets, three unsuspecting businessmen try to get on a bus that is out of service. As
the viewer of this story, you sense they are doomed, clutch-
ing briefcases, yelling. They argue and bargain their way on;
then one looks up and sees the wave. They are stuck in traffic, inside a bus, and all their clever bargaining has put them
right there. Soon the wave will engulf them, too.

On one of my last days in Christchurch, I head out to the
airport to have lunch with Lou Sanson, head of Antarctica
New Zealand. Lou wants to try a restaurant recently opened
in a nearby vineyard. As we walk to his car, decorated with
ANZ's emperor penguin logo, construction workers pass us
carrying metal beams. Lou's building also houses the U.S.
National Science Foundation polar program, and their second-floor offices are being secured against a terrorist attack,
metal detectors, special glass for the windows, the new architecture of these times.

It is an unusually hot day for autumn in Christchurch, and
we sip rosé on a slate patio while Lou talks about Antarctica's ice.

"Three of the continent's biggest glaciers, around Pine
Island in West Antarctica, are going fast. Estimates are they
are decreasing by about 250 cubic kilometers a year. This could
be part of their natural cycle. But the simultaneous melting
suggests something else might be happening."

I wonder if Lou senses when we could expect to know a bit

more. "The last time this happened was a hundred thousand years ago." He smiles and adds that a lot of focused research offered the promise of a better handle on the situation.

What would it mean? I ask, although I know the answer, because I had read about this possibility in a report.

"Sea level rises five meters over a couple hundred years, but more importantly, the East Antarctic Ice Sheet destabilizes and that contains enough ice to raise sea levels fifty meters. It would take another ice age to reverse that sort of meltdown." It is nothing to be alarmed about, he adds. "We just need to keep working in Antarctica to figure out what is going on."

A model of the Earth if East Antarctica's huge ice dome melts looks like this: Florida vanishes; London is under water, as is much of the east coast of England; in southeast Asia, Bangkok, Rangoon, and Ho Chi Minh City exist no more.

And then I am home, sitting in my living room in the dunes above the Pacific. On the wall, I have the map, titled "Ross Sea Region," Orsman gave me. The walls are painted Arctic blue, very pale, and the map of Antarctica, framed and about three-feet square, seems at home here. I stand before the map and study the perimeter, some names go like this, "Ice Shelf (Extent and shape of Bay Unknown)," and then my eye wanders to the Ross Sea, King Edward VII Land, Robert Scott Glacier, Amundsen Glacier, Shackleton Glacier. Empty space. One-third of the map is a 1:1,000,000 enlargement of Ross Island.

This is where I lived in 1988, almost twenty years ago. I reach my hand high on the glass, hear the Pacific crashing on Baker Beach, place my fingers on Ross Island, the ice tongue sketched in paler blue, the land the color of milky coffee. Cape Evans and the Barne Glacier. How I love the white, reflective, linear Barne Glacier, love it and feel its angles with my

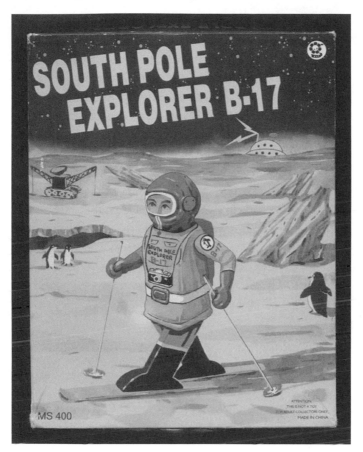

Polar Explorer toy box.

mouth and toes. I see the seal I hung out with at Cape Evans, near the Scott Hut, the one that liked to wiggle along then sit and stare out at sea, a visitation I broke when someone from Greenpeace saw me doing this and yelled out, "That seal will bite you like a rabid dog."

I think of Antarctica every day. Its demise, slow and fast, haunts me. On a windy winter afternoon in San Francisco I read in a news story how satellite images show West Antarctica, the smaller lobe, often compared in size to Texas, losing ice 60 percent faster than ten years ago. What does this mean? Maybe it means time will compress, water will rise more quickly, and the word "abrupt" will be added permanently to the now-common string of words, global climate change. As I read, lemon and ash-gray clouds arranged themselves over the Pacific Ocean and I recalled how Frank Arthur Worsley, who was the son of a bullock driver in New Zealand and may well offer the best model for toughing out bad weather, remarks in one of his books it was a pity that they were to perish because of the story that would be lost. I spin off my couch and outside to the dunes to feel the sea breeze, sharp and cold on my cheeks, closing my eyes, feet leave the ground, soaring out from land's end, make a left and I am heading home to Antarctica, embraced by the entire Earth and sky.

Bibliography

Archives

Canterbury Museum Archives

Susan Adams Papers. Letter from James Paton. Describes the trip down, depoting the various parties of the expedition, and discovering Amundsen in the Bay of Whales. MS 159, December 1910, 4 pp.

James Paton Papers. Rough log of the HMS *Morning*. MS 91.

Frank Arthur Worsley Papers, dated 1887–1943, relating to voyages on board *Countess of Ranfurly, George Cochrane, Kathleen Annie, Anna V,* and *Tyrconnel*; treasure hunting in the Cocos Islands and activities during World War II.

Correspondence on board the *Countess of Ranfurly,* Rarotonga, 1901; and on his experiences sailing around Rarotonga, January 1902. Carbon copies of contemporaneous typescripts. 40 pp. (several pages of final letter not extant). MS 539 Box 1, Item 1, and MS 540 2001.177.1–26.

Albert Armitage letter to Frank Worsley. 7 March 1933. Logbooks and papers relating to voyage of *Endurance* to Antarctica and return 1914–17, including original sketches of route across Elephant Island. Original and photographic reproduction made by Canterbury Museum. Red Cross Identification Card. Two standard boxes.

Workbook for log of *Endurance* from London to Weddell Sea, Antarctica, giving positional readings of ship, 1 August 1914–30 August 1915. 185 pp. Folder 1/Box 1 2001.177.1.

A hand-drawn map of King Haakon Bay and its surroundings and the course taken by the *James Caird* entering the bay, circa 1914. Signed by Worsley. 1 p. Folder 2/Box 1 2001.177.19.

Archives of New Zealand, Christchurch

Manuscript written by R. B. Thomson in April 1980 covering events that actually took place related to the "Erebus Disaster" up to that time. 178 pp. Accession No. 282.

Department of Scientific and Industrial Research,
Antarctic Division, 1980

Material related to the Royal Commission of Inquiry information prepared by R. B. Thomson indicating that McMurdo ATC [Air Traffic Control] were not aware that intended flight would be over Mount Erebus.

Material related to the Royal Commission of Inquiry manuscript and photo prints by Alwyn Gordon Vette sent to R. B. Thomson for comment. (This later became book *Impact Erebus*.)

Material resulting from early investigations and other actions immediately following the Recovery Operation Report on the recovery operations of the DC-10 Crash on Mt Erebus—Hugh Logan, February 1980.

Messages, reports, and other material produced on the day of the disaster and during the recovery operation NZ Mountaineers who actually worked on DC10 crash site, Mt Erebus.

Department of Scientific and Industrial Research,
Antarctic Division, 1979

Pre-Erebus ANZ [Air New Zealand] flight plan February 15 & 22 1977.

Pre-Erebus extract from U.S. Antarctican Journal regarding comments made on Antarctic overflights.

Department of Scientific and Industrial Research,
Antarctic Division, No date

Pre-Erebus letter from Vern Mitchell, Special Projects Officer, Air New Zealand, to R. B. Thomson regarding arrangements for flight planned for 14 November 1978.

Department of Scientific and Industrial Research,
Antarctic Division, 1978

Pre-Erebus list of flight crew NZ901 21 November 1979.

Department of Scientific and Industrial Research,
Antarctic Division, 1977

Pre-Erebus news release dated 14 January 1977 from Trans Tours on first flight.

Pre Erebus transcript of tape recording by R. B. Thomson (in-flight commentator) of first Air New Zealand flight to Antarctica on 15 February 1977. 38 pp.

Pre-Erebus U.S. air facilities in Antarctica—radio frequencies and charts of air-landing facilities.

Department of Scientific and Industrial Research,
Antarctic Division, No date

Pre-Erebus U.S. Policy Statement on support of aviation in Antarctica (26 June 1968).

Published Works

Alexander, Caroline. *The Endurance: Shackleton's Legendary Antarctic Expedition.* New York: Harper, 1997.

———. *Mrs. Chippy's Last Expedition.* New York: Harper, 1997.

Antarctica New Zealand. 2005. Antarctica New Zealand. <www.antarcticanz.govt.nz>. Accessed 28 March 2005.

Barber, Noel. *The White Desert.* London: Hodder & Stoughton, 1958.

Billing, Graham. *Forbush and the Penguins.* London: Hodder, 1965.

Borchgrevink, Carsten. *First on the Antarctic Continent: Being an Account of the British Antarctic Expedition*. London: Newnes, 1901.

British Antarctic Survey. 2005. British Antarctic Survey. <www.antarc tica.ac.uk>. Accessed 15 February 2005.

Byrd, Richard E. *Alone*. Washington: Island Press, 2003.

Caesar, Adrian. *The White*. Sydney: Pan Macmillian, 1999.

Cherry-Garrard, Apsley. *The Worst Journey in the World*. London: Constable, 1922.

CIA Factbook: Antarctica. 2005. Central Intelligence Agency. <www.odci .gov/cia/publications/factbook>. Accessed 12 January 2005.

Connell, Evan S. *The White Lantern & Other Pursuits*. London: Pimlico, 2002.

Davies, Fiona. "Safe Return Doubtful." Exhibit prospectus for the Canterbury Museum. Unpublished.

Eiseley, Loren. *The Star Thrower*. New York: Harcourt, 1978.

Eliot, T. S. *Collected Poems: 1909–1962*. New York: Harcourt, 1963.

Fuchs, Vivian, and Edmund Hillary. *The Crossing of the Antarctic*. London: Cassell, 1958.

Gateway Antarctica. 2005. Gateway Antarctica, University of Canterbury. <www.anta.canterbury.ac.nz>. Accessed 13 May 2005.

Gurney, Alan. *Below the Convergence: Voyages toward Antarctica 1699–1839*. New York: Norton, 1997.

———. *The Race to the White Continent*. New York: Norton, 2000.

Gutkind, Lee, ed. *On Nature*. New York: Tarcher/Putnam, 2002.

Harrowfield, David L. *Icy Heritage: Historic Sites of the Ross Sea Region*. Christchurch: Antarctic Heritage Trust, 1995.

Headland, Robert. *Chronological List of Antarctic Expeditions and Related Historical Events*. Cambridge: Cambridge University Press, 1989.

Hillary, Peter, and John E. Elder. *In the Ghost Country*. Auckland: Random, 2004.

Huntford, Roland. Introduction to *The Shackleton Voyages: A Pictorial Anthology of the Polar Explorer and Edwardian Hero*. London: Weidenfeld & Nicolson, 2002.

———. *Scott and Amundsen*. London: Hodder & Stoughton, 1979.

———. *Shackleton*. London: Hodder & Stoughton, 1985.

Hurley, Frank. *Shackleton's Argonauts: The Epic Tale of Shackleton's Voyage to Antarctica in 1915*. 2nd ed. Auckland: Collins, 1979.

Isles. Robert. Memo to ANZ. Ross Sea, Antarctica. 2 February 2002.

———. Personal interview. January 2004.

Joyner, Christopher C. *Governing the Frozen Commons: The Antarctic Regime and Environmental Protection*. Columbia: University of South Carolina Press, 1998.

Keneally, Thomas. *Victim of the Aurora*. London: Collins Sons, 1977.

Lansing, Alfred. *Endurance: Shackleton's Incredible Voyage*. New York: Carroll & Graf, 1959.

Lopate, Phillip. *The Art of the Personal Essay*. New York: Doubleday, 1994.

Mahon, P. T., The Hon. *Verdict on Erebus*. Auckland: Fontana, 1985.

May, John. *Greenpeace Book of Antarctica*. London: Kindersley, 1988.

Mulvaney, Kieran. Afterword to *Alone*, by Richard E. Byrd. Washington: Island Press, 2003.

Nelson, Victoria. *The Secret Life of Puppets*. Cambridge: Harvard University Press, 2001.

Norris, Baden. *Antarctic Reflections*. Christchurch: New Zealand Antarctic Soc., n.d.

Orsman, Chris. *South*. London: Faber and Faber, 1999.

Peat, Neville. *Looking South*. Wellington: New Zealand Antarctic Soc., 1983.

Peterson, Roger Tory. *Penguins*. Boston: Houghton, 1979.

Poe, Edgar Allen. *The Narrative of Arthur Gordon Pym*. New York: Penguin, 1999.

Pynchon, Thomas. *V.* New York: Perennial Classics, 1999.

Quartermain, Leslie B. *South to the Early History of the Ross Sea Sector, Antarctica.* London: Oxford University Press, 1967.

Robinson, Kim Stanley. *Antarctica.* New York: Bantam, 1998.

Rubin, Jeff. *Antarctica.* Hawthorn: Lonely Planet, 1996.

Scholes, Arthur. *Seventh Continent.* London: Allen, 1953.

Schulthess, Emil. *Antarctica: A Photographic Survey.* New York: Simon and Schuster, 1960.

Scott, Robert. *Scott's Last Expedition.* London: Smith and Elder, 1913.

———. *The Voyage of the Discovery.* London: Smith and Elder, 1905.

Shackleton, Ernest H. *Aurora Australis.* Auckland: SeTo, 1988.

———. *The Heart of the Antarctic: the Farthest South Expedition 1907–1909.* 2nd ed. New York: Signet, 2000.

———. *South.* 2nd ed. London: Century, 1989.

Soloman, Susan. *The Coldest March.* New Haven: Yale University Press, 2001.

Soper, Tony. *Antarctica—A Guide to the Wildlife.* Old Saybrook CT: Globe Pequot Press, 1994.

Templeton, Malcolm. *Protecting Antarctica: The Development of the Treaty System.* Wellington: New Zealand Inst. of Intl. Affairs, 2002.

Thomson, David. *Scott's Men.* London: Lane, 1977.

Thomson, John. *Shackleton's Captain: A Bibliography of Frank Worsley.* Christchurch: Hazard Press, 1998.

Various authors. *Antarctica: The Extraordinary History of Man's Consequence of the Frozen Continent.* 2nd ed. Sydney: Reader's Digest, 1998.

Wegener, Alfred. *The Origin of Continents and Oceans.* Translated by John Biram from the 4th German ed. New York: Dover, 1966.

Wheeler, Sara. *Antarctica, the Falklands and South Georgia.* London: Cadogan, 1997.

———. *Cherry.* London: Vintage, 2002.

———. Introduction to *Shackleton's Boat Journey*, by F. A. Worsley. 2nd ed. London: Pimlico, 1999.

Wilson, Eric G. *The Spiritual History of Ice: Romanticism, Science, and the Imagination*. New York: Palgrave, 2003.

———. Appearance on *Odyssey*, Chicago Public Radio.

Wolfe, Richard. Personal Interview. October, 2003.

Worsley, F. A. "An Account of a Boat Journey from Elephant Island to South Georgia Island."

———. *The Blue Peter*. London. 1924.

———. *Endurance: An Epic of Polar Adventure*. 2nd ed. London: Norton, 2000.

———. *First Voyage*. 2nd ed. London: Lowe and Brydone, 1947.

———. *Shackleton's Boat Journey*. 2nd ed. London: Pimlico, 1999